CAKE POPS

by *Bakerella*

CAKE POPS

BY *Bakerella*

Tips, Tricks, and Recipes for More Than 40 Irresistible Mini Treats

By Angie Dudley

CHRONICLE BOOKS
SAN FRANCISCO

Dedication

For Mady, with love.

This book is further dedicated to the readers of bakerella.com. Your enthusiasm and excitement for making these little treats inspires me every day. I hope you enjoy this book as much as I did writing it for you.

Acknowledgments

Mom—Thank you for always being there for me, for being my best friend, and being the best taste-tester around.

Jill Brown—I'm so glad you introduced me to cake balls at Rosa's party. Thank you. This is all your fault.

Angie Mosier—Your introductory cake decorating class was so inspiring. Thank you for putting a smile on my face that I can't get rid of.

Laura Celentano—Thank you for sharing my cupcake pops with Martha Stewart, and to Martha herself—thank you for the amazing opportunity to be on your show.

Danny and Monica—You've listened to me for the last two years talk about cake pops. Thank you for that and for encouraging me every step of the way. Monica—thanks for helping test recipes, and Danny—thanks for designing such cute tags.

Amy Treadwell—My editor, thank you and the entire Chronicle team—including designer, Anne Donnard; managing editor, Doug Ogan; production coordinator, Tera Killip; marketing team, Peter Perez and David Hawk; and copy editor, Rebecca Pepper—for taking my words and photos and turning them into such a beautiful book.

Ree, The Pioneer Woman—I can't thank you enough for inviting me to the ranch for a cake pop party and demo. Your generosity and kindness has meant so much to me.

Spitfire Studios—Tom, thanks for giving me your studio, your time, and talent for several days. I'm sure you'll never look at sprinkles the same again. Boxley—thanks for all your help. Nicole—thank you, too.

Family and friends—Thanks for being so excited with me, and I love you all.

Library of Congress Cataloging-in-Publication Data available.

ISBN 978-0-8118-7637-7

Manufactured in China.

Designed by Anne Donnard
Typesetting by RISE-AND-SHINE STUDIO

20 19 18 17 16 15 14

Chronicle Books LLC
680 Second Street
San Francisco, California 94107
www.chroniclebooks.com

Contents

- Introduction 6

THE METHODS 9
- Basic Cake Balls 11
- Basic Cake Pops 15
- Basic Cupcake Pops 19
- Basic Cupcake Bites 25
- Troubleshooting 28

THE TECHNIQUES 29
  Cake Pop Flavor Combinations 30
  Crumbling Your Cake 30
  Creating Shapes 32
  Candy Coating Basics 32
  Dipping Methods 36
  My Two Favorite Tools 39
  Main Ingredients 40
  Equipment 40
  Sprinkles 42
  Decorative Add-Ons 42

CAKE POP PROJECTS 47
- Sweet Hearts 49
- Spring Fling 51
- Spring Chicks 53
- Pastel Bunny Pops 55
- Sugar Sheep 57
- Confetti Easter Eggs 59
- Easter Baskets 61
- Clowning Around 63
- Ice Cream Cone Sundaes 67

- Chocolate Cupcake Pops 69
- Popcorn Bags 73
- Apple Pops 75
- Strawberry Patch Pops 77
- Bride & Groom Cake Pops 79
- Baby Faces 81
- Graduation Caps 83
- Pool Party Pops 85
- Martians 89
- Robots 91
- Monster Pops 93
- Pirate Pops 95
- Game Ball Cupcake Bites 97
- Lovely Little Ladybugs 99
- Froggies 103
- Barnyard Friends: 105
  Pink Piggies 105
  Cow Pops 106
  Chickens 107
- Puppy Pops 108
- Lions, Tigers & Bears, Oh My! 111
  Little Lions 111
  Tiny Tigers 113
  Brown Bears 114
- Koala Bears 117
- Panda Bears 119
- Monkey Business 121
- Black Cats 123
- Jack-o'-Lanterns 125

- Ghostly Goodies 127
- Spooky Witches 129
- Yummy Mummies 131
- Owls 133
- Turkey Time 135
- Hanukkah Pops 137
- Reindeer 139
- Simple Santa Hats 141
- Cheery Christmas Trees 143
- Sweet Snowmen 145

CAKE & FROSTING RECIPES 147
- Cake Recipes 148
  Yellow Cake 148
  Chocolate Cake 148
- Frosting Recipes 149
  Vanilla Frosting 149
  Cream Cheese Frosting 149
  Chocolate Frosting 149
  Chocolate Cream Cheese Frosting 149

DISPLAYING, STORING, SHIPPING
& SUPPLIES 151
  Displaying Your Cake Pops 152
  Storing and Shipping Cake Pops 154
- Supplies 155
- Cake Pops Projects Photo Index .. 156
- Index 157
- Table of Equivalents 160

◎ Introduction

Welcome to Cake Pops! I'm not a professional baker, and I don't have any formal training in chocolate or pastries or anything confectionery. But I do have a passion to learn and a desire to try new things. I've always loved sweets, and my motto has always been "the more chocolate, the better!" But growing up, I never really experimented with anything other than packaged cake, cookie, or brownie mixes. It never even crossed my mind that I could or should try to bake from scratch. Yellow cake mix and chocolate frosting were the extent of my cake-baking adventures (and they're still a favorite combination today).

On a whim in 2007, I took a two-hour cake decorating class. We learned how to make and tint homemade frosting, properly ice cakes, and use decorator bags and tips. You know— the basics. Well, that class changed everything for me. I still remember how happy I was to be exposed to the world of cake decorating. Even now, that feeling is still with me and inspires me to keep baking. To branch out and expand my experiences. To try new things without being afraid of the outcome. It's only sugar, you know. Even mistakes can be sweet!

Several months after finishing the cake class, I started a blog to chronicle my baking attempts. I named it Bakerella (www.bakerella.com), the same as my user name on Flickr.com, where I was hosting my photographs. I didn't tell anyone about my site in the beginning. I started out with some of my favorite things to make . . . and cake balls were one of them. I was introduced to cake balls at a Christmas party by my best friend's mother-in-law. One thing led to another, and over time I turned the bite-size balls of cake into cake pops and then developed them further into cupcake-shaped cake pops. The cupcake pops took the Internet by storm and caught the attention of *The Martha Stewart Show*. Before I knew it, my anonymous blog had catapulted me onto national TV to show Martha herself how to create the tiny treats. Needless to say, my friends and family were a little surprised.

Since the show, I have received so many wonderful e-mails and messages from readers about how the blog has inspired them to start baking. Readers began re-creating my cake and cupcake pops and sharing their photos with me. The excitement surrounding the pops made me want to experiment even more, which led to this book, where I share more than forty cake pop projects, plus techniques for creating your own.

So, get ready to experience cake as you've never seen (or eaten) it before. You won't find any traditional layer cakes or cupcakes in this book, but you will find ideas for amazingly creative bites of individually decorated cakes, and frosting.

Need something unique for a birthday party, baby shower, wedding, or upcoming holiday? The answer is right here. Let cake pops be the stars at your next event or party. But be careful: once you make them, you won't want to stop, and anyone who tries them probably won't let you.

Don't worry. You don't have to be a pastry artist or confectionery genius to make cake pops. You don't even need to be a great baker. With a few ingredients and common candy, you can transform any cake, even a store-bought one, into fascinating tiny treats.

You'll learn the methods behind the madness. You'll see how easy cake pops are to decorate. You'll learn techniques that will kick-start your creativity. Once you make your first cake pops, you'll be so proud of what you've accomplished. I promise.

I hope you enjoy them and find the same passion as I have, no matter what the subject!

Are you ready to get started?

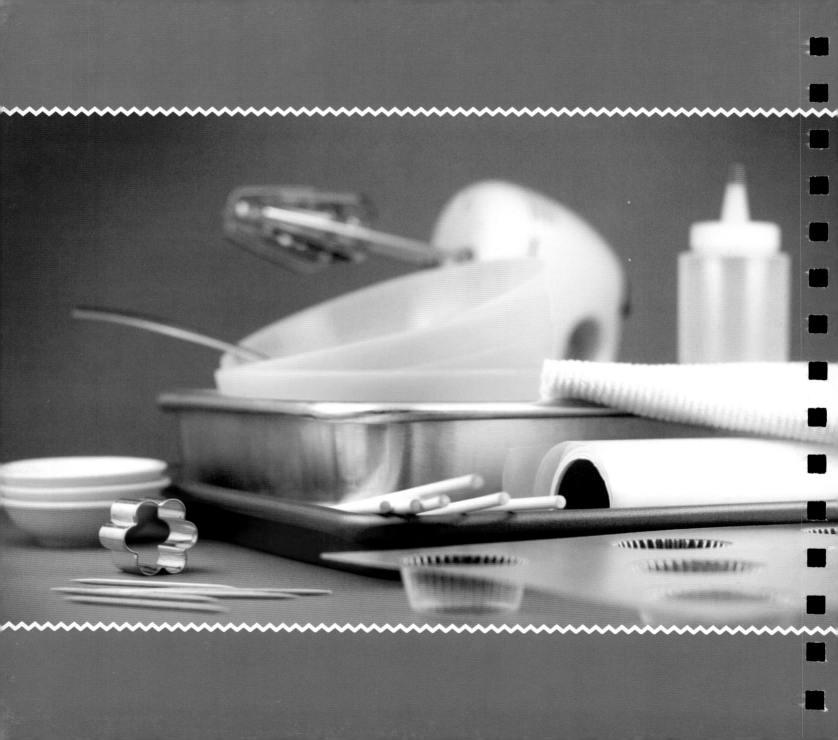

The Methods

Cake pops, cupcake pops, cake balls, and bites. They all have the same things in common: cake, frosting, candy, and cute. But these aren't ordinary cakes. They are tiny candy-covered confections made of crumbled cake mixed with frosting that you can mold into different shapes and decorate for any occasion. They are super-sweet, extremely moist, and completely covered in candy coating.

Over the next few pages, you'll find easy instructions that will help you master each of the four methods of creating unique sweet treats. Get ready to impress your friends, your family, and even yourself.

The following how-to's are based on using a cake mix and ready-made frosting. It's a really easy way to learn the basics and achieve predictable, consistent results. Then, once you feel comfortable making and decorating your very own cake pops, you'll have the knowledge to branch out with other cake and frosting recipes and get even more creative with custom flavors.

Or just stick with the mixes. I do.

Refer to page 30 for suggested cake mix and ready-made frosting combinations and pages 148 to 149 for easy cake and frosting recipes from scratch.

Basic Cake Balls

Cake balls are bite-size balls made of crumbled cake mixed with frosting and covered in candy coating. They are super-easy to make and form the basis of endless variations of decorated cake pops, cupcake pops, and cake bites.

MAKES 48 CAKE BALLS

YOU'LL NEED

18.25-ounce box cake mix

9-by-13-inch cake pan

Large mixing bowl

16-ounce container ready-made frosting

Large metal spoon

Wax paper

2 baking sheets

Plastic wrap

32 ounces (2 pounds) candy coating

Deep, microwave-safe plastic bowl

Toothpicks

Resealable plastic bag or squeeze bottle (optional)

Bake the cake as directed on the box, using a 9-by-13-inch cake pan. Let cool completely.

Once the cake is cooled, get organized and set aside plenty of time (at least an hour) to crumble, roll, and dip 4 dozen cake balls.

Crumble the cooled cake into a large mixing bowl. See "Crumbling Your Cake" on page 30. You should not see any large pieces of cake.

Add three-quarters of the container of frosting. (You will not need the remaining frosting.) Mix it into the crumbled cake, using the back of a large metal spoon, until thoroughly combined. If you use the entire container, the cake balls will be too moist.

The mixture should be moist enough to roll into 1½-inch balls and still hold a round shape. After rolling the cake balls by hand, place them on a wax paper–covered baking sheet.

Cover with plastic wrap and chill for several hours in the refrigerator, or place in the freezer for about 15 minutes. You want the balls to be firm but not frozen.

If you're making a project that calls for uncoated cake balls, stop here and proceed to decorate the cake balls, following the project instructions.

(continued)

The first time I tried a cake ball was at a Christmas party in 2005. The appearance of the balls was deceptive—they looked like peanut butter balls—and I almost passed them by. But then I was told they weren't peanut butter balls at all, but cake balls. Well, the name alone sent me straight over to investigate. And I'm so glad I did, because they have been a featured sweet at many family get-togethers since and the basis for my cake-pop craze.

Place the candy coating in a deep, microwave-safe plastic bowl. These bowls make it easier to cover the cake balls completely with candy coating while holding the bowl without burning your fingers. (I usually work with about 16 ounces of coating at a time.)

Melt the candy coating, following the instructions on the package. Microwave on medium power for 30 seconds at a time, stirring with a spoon in between. You can also use a double boiler. Either way, make sure you do not overheat the coating. See "Candy Coating Basics," page 32, for more on working with candy coating.

Now you're ready to coat. Take a few cake balls at a time out of the refrigerator or freezer to work with. If they're in the freezer, transfer the rest of the balls to the refrigerator at this point, so they stay firm but do not freeze.

Place one ball at a time into the bowl of candy coating. Spoon extra coating over any uncoated areas of the cake ball to make sure it is completely covered in candy coating. Then lift out the cake ball with your spoon. Avoid stirring it in the coating, because cake crumbs can fall off into the coating.

Holding the spoon over the bowl, tap the handle of the spoon several times on the edge of the bowl until the excess coating falls off and back into the bowl. This technique also creates a smooth surface on the outside of the cake ball.

Transfer the coated cake ball to the second wax paper–covered baking sheet to dry. Let the coated cake ball slide right off the spoon. Some coating may pool around the base of the ball onto the wax paper. If so, simply take a toothpick and use it to draw a line around the base of the cake ball before the coating sets. Once the coating sets, you can break off any unwanted coating.

Repeat with the remaining cake balls and let dry completely.

If you have extra candy coating left over, pour it into a resealable plastic bag (and then snip off the corner) or into a squeeze bottle and drizzle it over the tops in a zigzag motion to decorate.

You can make the cake balls ahead of time and store them in an air-tight container on the counter or in the refrigerator for several days.

Tips

- The cake balls will be easier to roll if you wash and dry your hands periodically during the rolling process. Dry your hands completely each time, and make sure you don't get water in the candy coating, as that can make it unusable.

- You can use a mini ice-cream scoop to get uniform-size cake balls.

- If you don't need or want to make 48 cake balls, simply divide the cake in half for 24 cake balls or in quarters for 12 and freeze the remaining cake for later use. Remember to reduce the amount of frosting proportionally.

It took me a while before I realized that candy coating came in various colors and flavors. One day I stumbled across pink candy coating at a craft store, and that's when everything changed. My eyes opened to the possibilities. I thought how cute it would be to turn cake balls into cake lollipops . . . or cake pops for short. The cake pops in this photo are the first ones I ever attempted. I had no idea at the time that they would inspire a cake pop sensation.

Basic Cake Pops

Cake pops are based on the same idea as cake balls, with the addition of a lollipop stick and a different approach to dipping. The lollipop sticks increase the cuteness factor, making them perfect for party favors and gifts.

MAKES 48 CAKE POPS

YOU'LL NEED

18.25-ounce box cake mix

9-by-13-inch cake pan

Large mixing bowl

16-ounce container ready-made frosting

Large metal spoon

Wax paper

2 baking sheets

Plastic wrap

48 ounces (3 pounds) candy coating

Deep, microwave-safe plastic bowl

48 paper lollipop sticks

Styrofoam block (see page 41)

Bake the cake as directed on the box, using a 9-by-13-inch cake pan. Let cool completely.

Once the cake is cooled, get organized and set aside plenty of time (a couple of hours) to crumble, roll, and dip 4 dozen cake pops.

Crumble the cooled cake into a large mixing bowl. See "Crumbling Your Cake" on page 30. You should not see any large pieces of cake.

Add three-quarters of the container of frosting. (You will not need the remaining frosting.) Mix it into the crumbled cake, using the back of a large metal spoon, until thoroughly combined. If you use the entire container, the cake balls will be too moist.

The mixture should be moist enough to roll into 1½-inch balls and still hold a round shape. After rolling the cake balls by hand, place them on wax paper–covered baking sheets.

Cover with plastic wrap and chill for several hours in the refrigerator, or place in the freezer for about 15 minutes. You want the balls to be firm but not frozen.

Place the candy coating in a deep, microwave-safe plastic bowl. These bowls make it easier to cover the cake balls completely with candy coating while holding the bowl without burning your fingers. (I usually work with about 16 ounces of coating at a time.)

Melt the candy coating, following the instructions on the package. Microwave on medium power for 30 seconds at a time, stirring with a spoon in between. You can also use a double boiler. Either way, make sure you do not overheat the coating. See "Candy Coating Basics," page 32, for more on working with candy coating.

Now you're ready to dip. Take a few cake balls at a time out of the refrigerator or freezer to work with. If they're in the freezer, transfer the rest of the balls to the refrigerator at this point, so they stay firm but do not freeze.

One at a time, dip about ½ inch of the tip of a lollipop stick into the melted candy coating, and then insert the lollipop stick straight into a cake ball, pushing it no more than halfway through.

(continued)

Holding the lollipop stick with cake ball attached, dip the entire cake ball into the melted candy coating until it is completely covered, and remove it in one motion. Make sure the coating meets at the base of the lollipop stick. This helps secure the cake ball to the stick when the coating sets. The object is to completely cover the cake ball and remove it without submerging it in the coating more than once. A small, deep plastic bowl is very helpful during this step. If you do resubmerge the cake pop, the weight of the candy coating can pull on the cake ball and cause it to get stuck in the coating.

The thinner the consistency of your coating, the easier it will be to coat the cake pops. If you find that your coating is too thick, add some shortening or paramount crystals (see page 40) to help thin it and make the coating more fluid.

When you remove the cake pop from the candy coating, some excess coating may start to drip. Hold the cake pop in one hand and use the other hand to gently tap the first wrist. Rotate the lollipop stick if necessary to allow the excess coating to fall off evenly, so one side doesn't get heavier than the other. If you didn't completely dunk the cake pop, this method of tapping and rotating generally takes care of that. The coating will slowly slide down the surface of the cake ball until it reaches the lollipop stick.

If too much coating surrounds the base of the lollipop stick, you can wipe the excess off with your finger. Simply place your finger on the stick right under the cake ball and spin the lollipop stick, allowing any excess coating to fall off and back into the bowl of coating. When most of the excess coating has fallen off and it is no longer dripping, stick the cake pop into the prepared Styrofoam block (see Tips).

Repeat with the remaining cake balls and let dry completely.

Store the cake pops in an airtight container on the counter or in the refrigerator for several days. You can also cover them in small treat bags, tied with a ribbon, and leave them in the Styrofoam block on the counter.

Tips

- Make the cake the day before and let it cool overnight.

- Use a toothpick to encourage the coating to cover any small exposed areas or to make sure it surrounds the lollipop stick.

- Make sure the cake balls are chilled and firm when you dip them. If they are room temperature, they are likely to fall off the lollipop sticks into the melted candy coating. You can always place them back in the freezer for a few minutes to quickly firm them up again.

- Poke holes in the Styrofoam block before you start dipping the pops. Just use one of the lollipop sticks to make holes about 2 inches apart.

- For fun, experiment with different colors of candy coating.

- Cake pops need more attention and therefore a little more time to complete than the cake balls. Set aside a couple of hours.

- When using the cake pop method, you can also make the balls in different shapes. Just roll them into balls, place in the freezer or refrigerator to firm, and then mold into your desired shape.

Basic Cupcake Pops

Not only can you make cake balls and turn them into cake pops, but you can also mold them into other shapes using a small metal cookie cutter. For these cupcake pops, use a flower-shaped cookie cutter. Take them to the next level of cuteness by using more than one color of candy coating and adding sprinkles and candy for decoration.

MAKES 48 CUPCAKE POPS

YOU'LL NEED

18.25-ounce box cake mix

9-by-13-inch cake pan

Large mixing bowl

16-ounce container ready-made frosting

Large metal spoon

Wax paper

2 baking sheets

Plastic wrap

Flower-shaped cookie cutter (1¼ inches wide by ¾ inch deep)

32 ounces (2 pounds) chocolate candy coating

2 deep, microwave-safe plastic bowls

Dish towel

48 paper lollipop sticks

16 ounces pink candy coating

Toothpicks

M&M's or similarly shaped candy

Sprinkles

Styrofoam block (see page 41)

Bake the cake as directed on the box, using a 9-by-13-inch cake pan. Let cool completely.

Once the cake is cooled, get organized and set aside plenty of time (a few hours) to crumble, roll, shape, dip, and decorate 4 dozen cupcake pops.

Crumble the cooled cake into a large bowl. See "Crumbling Your Cake" on page 30. You should not see any large pieces of cake.

(continued)

> **After I discovered that candy coatings came in so many colors, I was eager to experiment.**
> The cake pops are cute, but I wanted to make them even cuter. Turning them into cupcakes was the obvious next step for me. One day an idea came in the form of a cookie cutter I had lying around the kitchen, and I developed this little technique for shaped cakes that I call cupcake pops. The response was overwhelming, from an invitation to appear on *The Martha Stewart Show* to the many messages from the wonderfully sweet readers of Bakerella .com who shared their excitement of learning to make these treats.

Add three-quarters of the container of frosting. (You will not need the remaining frosting.) Mix it into the crumbled cake, using the back of a large metal spoon, until thoroughly combined. If you use the entire container, the cake balls will be too moist.

The mixture should be moist enough to roll into 1½-inch balls and still hold a round shape. After rolling the cake balls by hand, place them on a wax paper–covered baking sheet.

Cover with plastic wrap and chill for several hours in the refrigerator, or place in the freezer for about 15 minutes. You want the balls to be firm but not frozen.

Remove the baking sheet from the refrigerator or freezer and begin shaping the cake balls into cupcakes. Take a chilled ball and roll it into a cylinder shape. Then slide it into the flower-shaped cookie cutter. The cake mixture should fill the entire cutter, with any excess forming a mounded cupcake top on one side. You can use your thumb to keep the shape flat on one side, allowing the rest to form a mound on the other. When you have the shape the way you like it, gently push the shaped cupcake out of the cutter from the bottom. If the mixture is still firm enough, you should also be able to gently pull it out by holding the top mounded side.

Place the cupcake-shaped cake ball, right-side up, back on the wax paper–covered baking sheet.

Continue with the remaining cake balls.

Once the balls are all shaped into cupcakes, return them to the freezer for 5 to 10 minutes to keep them firm.

Place the chocolate candy coating in a deep, microwave-safe plastic bowl. These bowls make it easier to dip the cupcake bottoms completely in candy coating while holding the bowl without burning your fingers. (I usually work with about 16 ounces of coating at a time.)

Melt the chocolate candy coating, following the instructions on the package. Microwave on medium power for 30 seconds at a time, stirring with a spoon in between. You can also use a double boiler. Either way, make sure you do not overheat the coating. See "Candy Coating Basics," page 32, for more on working with candy coating.

Now you're ready to dip. Take a few cupcake-shaped balls at a time out of the refrigerator or freezer to work with. Transfer the rest to the refrigerator at this point, so they stay firm but do not freeze.

One at a time, take a cupcake-shaped cake ball and, holding it by the mounded top, dip the bottom into the melted chocolate candy coating—just to the point where the mounded shape starts. Remove it from the chocolate, turn it upside down, and swirl your hand in a circular motion. This will cause any excess chocolate coating to slide down. When the coating reaches the bottom of the mounded cupcake top, you can stop. Have a dish towel handy to wipe off your fingertips, as it is highly likely that you'll get some coating on them. Don't use water to rinse your hands, because getting water in the coating can make it unusable.

Place the half-coated cupcake shape on the second wax paper–covered baking sheet, chocolate-candy-coating-side up, mounded-side down. Immediately dip about ½ inch of the tip of a lollipop stick into the melted candy coating, and insert the stick straight into the flat, chocolate-coated bottom of the cupcake while the chocolate is still wet. Push it no more than halfway through.

Continue with the rest of the cupcake-shaped cake balls.

Allow the chocolate to dry completely.

Melt the pink candy coating in the same way that you melted the chocolate. You will now decorate the tops. This all comes together quickly, resulting in a finished cupcake pop.

(continued)

Holding its lollipop stick, dip the top of a cupcake in the melted pink candy coating. It should completely cover the rest of the exposed cupcake and meet the edge of the chocolate coating.

Remove the cupcake pop from the coating and turn it right-side up. If the coating is too hot, it will start to drip down the sides. If this happens, let the coating sit for a few minutes to cool and start to thicken. Then when you dip the tops, the coating will stay in place.

While the coating is still wet, use a toothpick to touch up any areas the coating may not have covered. Then place 1 M&M (M-side down) on the top and add sprinkles for decoration (see page 42).

Place the cupcake pop in a prepared Styrofoam block to dry completely. Repeat with the remaining cupcake pops.

Store the cupcake pops in an airtight container on the counter or in the refrigerator for several days. You can also cover them in small treat bags, tied with a ribbon, and leave them in the Styrofoam block on the counter.

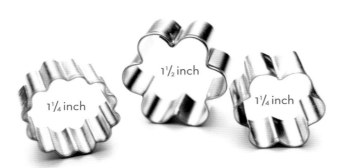

Tips

- Make the cake the day before and let it cool overnight. Then you can do the crumbling, rolling, shaping, dipping, and decorating on the second day.

- You can also leave uncoated cake balls, covered in plastic wrap, in the refrigerator overnight if you want to do the dipping on the following day.

- You can make these without lollipop sticks. They're just as cute.

- Don't get any water in the candy coating. Keep your hands completely dry. Water will mess up the coating and ruin all your hard work.

- Poke holes in the Styrofoam block before you start dipping, using a lollipop stick. Leave enough space between the holes so the cakes won't touch.

- Experiment with different candy coating color combinations.

- You can also use this technique with other small cookie cutters, such as hearts or butterflies (see pages 49 and 51).

- Place sprinkles in a small dish and pinch a few with your fingers to sprinkle on top of the pops. Sprinkle over a large bowl to reuse any that fall.

- To see a video demonstration of creating cupcake pops, go to www.marthastewart.com/recipe/cupcake-pops.

Basic Cupcake Bites

The cupcake pops are extremely popular, but these cupcake bites come in a close second. They rely on the use of a plastic candy mold to help form the shape of the cupcake bottom. No sticks. No tapping off excess coating. Just a neat, professional-looking finished product. And best of all, they're easy!

MAKES 48 CUPCAKE BITES

YOU'LL NEED

18.25-ounce box cake mix

9-by-13-inch cake pan

Large mixing bowl

16-ounce container ready-made frosting

Large metal spoon

Wax paper

2 baking sheets

Plastic wrap

48 ounces (3 pounds) chocolate candy coating

2 deep, microwave-safe plastic bowls

Large plastic squeeze bottle

Medium-sized plastic candy cup mold (with cavity openings 1$\frac{1}{2}$ inches wide)

24 ounces purple candy coating

Toothpicks

M&M's or similarly shaped candy

Sprinkles

Bake the cake as directed on the box, using a 9-by-13-inch cake pan. Let cool completely.

Once the cake is cooled, get organized and set aside plenty of time (a couple of hours) to crumble, roll, dip, and decorate 4 dozen cupcake bites.

Crumble the cooled cake into a large bowl. See "Crumbling Your Cake" on page 30. You should not see any large pieces of cake.

Add three-quarters of the container of frosting. (You will not need the remaining frosting.) Mix it into the crumbled cake, using the back of a large metal spoon, until thoroughly combined. If you use the entire container, the cake balls will be too moist.

The mixture should be moist enough to roll into 1$\frac{1}{2}$-inch balls and still hold a round shape. After rolling the cake balls by hand, place on a wax paper–covered baking sheet.

Cover with plastic wrap and chill for several hours in the refrigerator, or place in the freezer for about 15 minutes. You want the balls to be firm but not frozen.

If you're making a project that calls for uncoated cupcake bites, stop here and proceed to decorate the cupcake bites, following the project instructions.

(continued)

When visiting the candy-making sections in craft and cake supply stores, I began to pay attention to the various candy molds that are available. When I saw one for candy cups, I immediately thought it would be perfect to replicate baking cup liners. I love the ease of this method.

Place the chocolate candy coating in a deep, microwave-safe plastic bowl. (I usually work with about 16 ounces of coating at a time.) Melt the coating, following the instructions on the package. Microwave on medium power for 30 seconds at a time, stirring with a spoon in between. You can also use a double boiler. Either way, make sure you do not overheat the coating. See "Candy Coating Basics," page 32, for more on working with candy coating.

Once melted, transfer the chocolate coating to a large plastic squeeze bottle.

Use the squeeze bottle to fill one cavity of the candy mold about halfway full with chocolate coating, and immediately place a rolled cake ball into the coating. The cake ball should be slightly smaller than the width of the candy mold. Slowly push the cake ball down until the pressure causes the candy coating to force its way up the mold and fill in around the sides of the cake ball. You may have to experiment with a couple to get the right amount of chocolate coating. Stop pushing once the chocolate coating reaches the top edge of the candy mold, so that it doesn't form a lip around the edge. Repeat for the remaining cavities.

Set the filled candy mold tray on the second baking sheet to keep it from bending, and place in the freezer for just a few minutes to let the chocolate set.

Remove the tray from the freezer and separate the half-coated cupcake bites from the candy mold. Give the mold a twist and pull on the exposed cake ball.

Melt the purple candy coating in a microwave-safe plastic bowl to be used for the cupcake bite tops.

Holding the bottom of a cupcake bite, dip the top in the melted purple candy coating until it meets the edge of the chocolate coating. When removed, if the purple coating doesn't meet where the chocolate coating ends, you can turn it right-side up and swirl your hand in a circular motion to allow the purple coating to slowly work its way down the side of the mounded cupcake top. You can also use a toothpick to touch up any uncoated areas.

Immediately decorate with 1 M&M (M-side down) and some sprinkles and return to the wax paper–covered cookie sheet to dry completely. Repeat with the remaining cupcake bites.

Store in an airtight container on the counter or in the refrigerator for several days.

Tips

- The small ridges formed in the chocolate by the candy mold can melt when handled for too long. Wear cloth candy gloves to help prevent fingerprints when dipping the tops.

- You can use more than one candy mold to speed up the process.

- Experiment with different candy coating color combinations for the tops and bottoms of the cupcake bites.

Troubleshooting

You followed the directions but still need a little more help. Take a look at some of the following scenarios to see if you can find the answer.

Your cake is too moist and will not hold its shape when rolled into a ball. You probably used too much frosting in proportion to cake. Add more cake to balance it out. Try crumbling in a few store-bought cupcakes, minus the frosting.

Your coating won't cover the cake ball smoothly. Make sure the balls are firm and not frozen. Frozen cake balls mixed with hot candy coating will cause the coating to start to set too quickly, often before the cake ball can be coated properly. If your cake balls are chilled properly and the coating still won't cover them smoothly, make sure you are using the appropriate dipping technique (see page 36).

You can't find candy coating. Try melting regular chocolate, and use shortening or paramount crystals (see page 40) to make it easier for dipping. This is best used when making cake balls, because chocolate does not set as hard as candy coating does, making it less suitable for supporting cake pops on their sticks.

You made cake pops and the coating cracked. You may have rolled the cake balls too tightly. And if placed in the freezer too long, the cake may have tried to expand, resulting in a crack in the coating. Don't worry; they won't fall off the stick if they've been secured by coating at the base. And you can even dip them a second time to fix up the coating or drizzle and decorate in a way to disguise the crack. I've seen this happen with cake pops, but not with cupcake pops or bites, because these methods use a two-part dipping method and give the cake ball time to breathe before being coated.

Your candy coating is too thick. Don't turn up the heat. Making the candy coating hotter doesn't make it thinner. If your coating is melted and is still too thick, add shortening or paramount crystals (see page 40) until it is thin enough to work with.

Your cake pops fall off the sticks. Make sure the shaped cake balls are firm but not frozen when you dip. If they start to get soft, just return them to the freezer for a few minutes to firm them up. Make sure the coating is thin enough to dip and remove in one motion. Don't stir the cake pops in the coating. Make sure you don't insert sticks more than halfway through the cake pops. Finally, check that the coating surrounds the cake ball at the base where the lollipop stick is inserted. Use a toothpick if necessary to direct the coating around the base of the stick.

Cake or oil is trying to push its way out of the pop. Make sure the pop is completely coated. Even the tiniest opening will invite the cake to try and escape.

Cake crumbs are getting mixed in with the candy coating. The cake balls may not be firm enough. Chill them a little longer before dipping. If you use dark-colored cake, with lighter-colored candy coating, some crumbs may show up anyway. If so, redip them in a new batch of melted candy coating. This happens more often when making cake balls rather than cake pops. Make sure you do not stir cake balls in the bowl of candy coating. Drop them in, cover with more coating using a spoon, and then lift them out.

You can see your cake through the candy coating. When you use dark cake and light-colored candy coating, this can happen. To make the coating more opaque, dip the cake balls a second time.

Your candy coating has a grayish, filmy-looking surface. "Bloom" can be caused by improper storage of candy coating or changes in temperature when shipping. To avoid this, properly store your coatings in a cool, dry place away from direct heat or sunlight and avoid temperature changes. When purchasing candy coating from a store, pick out the package with the least amount of bloom, to get off to a good start. FYI: Coatings affected by bloom may not be as pretty, but they are still safe to eat.

The Techniques

Plan Ahead. Being organized will save you a lot of time and unnecessary frustration. You don't want to be counting out candies for decorating when you're dipping cake pops. Make sure everything is within easy reach. Sprinkles can go in small dishes, and lollipop sticks can stand in a small glass. You can also make the cake the night before and let it cool. Then your time the next day can be devoted to dipping and decorating.

Take some time and read through the following pages before you begin a cake-pop project, and you'll be on your way to becoming a pop star. When you finish a project, refer to pages 152 to 154 for presentation and storage ideas.

For more cake-pop designs from the readers of Bakerella.com, visit www.bakerella.com/pop-stars.

CAKE POP FLAVOR COMBINATIONS

Cake pops can be made in any number of cake and frosting combinations. Here are a few common cake mix and frosting suggestions, along with candy coating flavors, to get you started.

Chocolate Cake:	Frosting: Buttercream, vanilla, cream cheese, chocolate
	Coating: Milk chocolate, dark chocolate, vanilla, peanut butter, mint, butterscotch
Red Velvet Cake:	Frosting: Buttercream, vanilla, cream cheese
	Coating: Milk chocolate, dark chocolate, vanilla
White Cake:	Frosting: Buttercream, vanilla, cream cheese
	Coating: Milk chocolate, dark chocolate, vanilla, peanut butter, mint, butterscotch
Vanilla Cake:	Frosting: Buttercream, vanilla, cream cheese
	Coating: Milk chocolate, dark chocolate, vanilla, peanut butter, mint, butterscotch
Yellow Cake:	Frosting: Buttercream, vanilla, cream cheese
	Coating: Milk chocolate, dark chocolate, vanilla
Lemon Cake:	Frosting: Buttercream, vanilla, cream cheese, lemon
	Coating: Milk chocolate, dark chocolate, vanilla
Strawberry Cake:	Frosting: Buttercream, vanilla, cream cheese, strawberry
	Coating: Milk chocolate, dark chocolate, vanilla
Carrot Cake:	Frosting: Buttercream, vanilla, cream cheese
	Coating: Milk chocolate, dark chocolate, vanilla
Spice Cake:	Frosting: Buttercream, vanilla, cream cheese
	Coating: Milk chocolate, dark chocolate, vanilla

Light-colored frostings work better with light-colored cakes. The frosting blends right in and disappears.

But don't stop there. Adapt your own cake recipe. Just use the methods as a guide for the proportions. (These methods call for the equivalent of one 9-by-13-inch baked cake and three-fourths of a 16-ounce can of ready-made frosting. Avoid whipped frostings.) If your homemade cake and frosting recipe makes more or less than that, adjust the amount of frosting you add—more for larger cakes and less for smaller ones. And if you add too much frosting, don't worry. Just add more cake to balance out the proportions. Store-bought unfrosted cakes work in an emergency.

You can also use one of the recipes for homemade cakes and frostings provided on pages 148 to 149.

CRUMBLING YOUR CAKE

There are two main ways to crumble your cake and prepare it to be combined with frosting. The first, and handiest, is to just use, well, your hands. This method works great with cake mixes. The texture of the cake causes it to crumble easily. Just cut a baked 9-by-13-inch cake into four equal sections. Remove a section from the pan, break it in half, and rub the two pieces together over a large bowl, making sure to crumble any large pieces that fall off. You can also use a fork to break any larger pieces of cake apart. Repeat with each section until the entire cake is crumbled into a fine texture. If you have large pieces mixed in, the cake balls may turn out lumpy and bumpy.

What if you've baked a cake from scratch? No problem. You can still crumble it using your hands. But because the texture of scratch cakes can vary so much, it may be easier to just toss small sections of the cake into a food processor. This will ensure that the texture is fine enough.

Then add the frosting and mix with a large spoon until the frosting absorbs into the cake and disappears. Using the back of your spoon is a quick way to make sure the two are thoroughly combined.

- Are 4 dozen cake pops too many? You can make as few as a dozen at a time. Each quarter section of cake yields about 12 cake pops. Remember to adjust the amount of frosting accordingly. Just freeze the extra cake quarter sections and save for later use.

- When using light-colored cakes, remove any brown edges before crumbling to avoid brown specks in your cake balls.

CREATING SHAPES

Crumbled cake mixed with frosting can easily be rolled by hand into round balls. It can also be molded into oval, rectangular, or triangular shapes. Subtle changes in shape can turn a Christmas tree into a bunny or a ghost into a skull. And even if you don't change the shape at all, you'll find that decorating with different add-ons and candies can transform a basic round shape into endless designs.

Here's a guide to the most commonly used shapes from the ideas in this book.

ROUND: Bears, lions, tigers, chicks, pigs, cows, cats, monsters, babies, reindeer, ice cream cones, game balls, koalas, pumpkins, frogs, puppies, ladybugs, turkeys, pandas, clowns, Easter baskets, graduation caps

OVAL: Sheep, mummies, witches, owls

RECTANGULAR: Popcorn bags, robots

BELL/PEAR: Ghosts, snowmen, skulls

ROUNDED TRIANGLES/CONES: Trees, Santa hats, Martians, strawberries, bunnies, apples

COOKIE CUTTER SHAPES: Cupcakes, butterflies, flowers, hearts

Tips

- Make round-shaped cake balls first, until you're sure you will end up with the appropriate number. If you start shaping right away, you can end up with pieces that are too big.

- It's helpful to place the cake balls in the freezer for a few minutes to firm them up before reshaping them.

- Don't roll the cake balls too tightly. They may try to expand after coating, which can cause the coating to crack.

CANDY COATING BASICS

Candy coating, also referred to as candy wafers, compound coatings, confectionery coating, candy melts, chocolate bark, and bark coating, is used in candy making. It can be used for dipping, in candy molds, or even in squeeze bottles for piping or drizzling. Candy coating comes in a variety of colors and flavors. It is easy to use and doesn't require tempering, as chocolate does. Just melt and use.

Store coatings in a cool, dry place until ready to use. Do not store in the refrigerator or freezer. If stored properly, leftover candy coatings can even be reheated and used again.

It doesn't hurt to keep an extra bag of candy coating on hand for the color you are using, just in case. You can always use it on a future project if you don't need it.

Melting Methods

To use candy coating, simply melt the amount you need and you're ready to go. Rather than melting all of the candy coating at once, I usually work with about 16 ounces at a time. Try one of the following methods to find the one that appeals to you most.

MICROWAVE: Melt candy coating in a microwave-safe bowl. Microwave on medium power in 30-second intervals, stirring in between. Repeat until the coating is completely melted. When you first stir, the coating will still be firm. That's okay; just keep repeating, making sure not to overheat the coating. If the coating gets too hot, it will thicken and become unusable. In addition, be sure not to let any water mix with the coating.

DOUBLE BOILER: I don't usually use this method because most of the time I melt more than one color of candy coating, and it's easier to use the microwave and work with smaller bowls. However, if you are using one color, the double boiler method is a great alternative. Fill the bottom section of a double boiler with water and bring to a simmer. Remove it from the heat and place candy coating in the top section. Stir continuously until completely melted and smooth.

WARMING TRAY: A warming tray allows you to use several oven-safe bowls at one time. Make sure they are small and deep enough for dipping. Turn the tray on low and you will be able to keep multiple colors melted.

Thinning Candy Coating

Working with candy coating can be lots of fun, but only if it is working with you. Sometimes the coating is too thick, making it more difficult to dip the cake pops. Darker-colored coatings sometimes have this problem. An easy way to thin the coating is to use a product called paramount crystals (see page 40 and photo above), adding a few pieces to the coating. Stir until melted and the coating is fluid. You can use regular shortening or vegetable oil as an alternative. Start by adding just a teaspoon. Stir in until melted. Add more as needed until the coating is fluid enough to work with easily.

Using Chocolate as a Coating Substitute

Regular chocolate can be used as a substitute for candy coating, but keep in mind that the coatings are made to do just that—coat. Baking chocolate and morsels will cover the cake balls but will not harden in the same way that candy coating will. Therefore, this alternative is best when making cake balls instead of cake pops, because the pops need a hard coating to give them extra stability on the sticks. You may also need to thin chocolate with shortening or paramount crystals to make it more fluid.

Coloring Candy Coating

Although candy coating comes in a variety of basic colors, sometimes you need to tint your own to get just the right shade. Tinting white candy coating is also a great alternative if you need only a small amount of one color and don't want to buy a whole package of coating. Add a few drops of candy coloring to start. Add more color, a few drops at a time, until you achieve the shade you desire. If you add too much color, you can lighten it by adding more white candy coating.

Make sure to use oil-based candy coloring and not regular food coloring, which contains water. Food coloring will ruin the coating.

Candy Coating Colors

In addition to candy coating flavors such as chocolate and peanut butter, vanilla candy coating is available in a rainbow of colors. Here is a side-by-side chart of coatings from three popular candy coating makers. All three offer many of the same colors; however, the shades may be slightly different.

Candy Coating Colors	Make 'n Mold	Merckens	Wilton
Milk chocolate flavored	•	•	•
Dark chocolate flavored	•	•	•
Peanut butter flavored	•	•	•
Butterscotch flavored		•	
White—vanilla flavored	•	•	•
Superwhite—vanilla flavored		•	
Light pink—vanilla flavored	•		•
Dark pink—vanilla flavored			
Orange—vanilla flavored	•	•	•
Yellow—vanilla flavored	•	•	•
Blue—vanilla flavored	•	•	•
Navy—vanilla flavored			
Light green—vanilla flavored	•	•	
Dark green—vanilla flavored	•	•	•
Red—vanilla flavored	•	•	
Orchid/lavender—vanilla flavored	•	•	
Peach—vanilla flavored		•	
Midnight black*—vanilla flavored			•

*Available for Halloween

Some candy coating colors are also available in mint flavor, including chocolate, white, green, and pink.

Keep in mind that dark-colored cakes may show through white or light-colored coatings. If you want the coating to be completely opaque, try dipping a second time.

Combine candy coating colors to create different colors or lighten any color by adding white candy melts.

Adding Flavorings

Besides adding color to your candy coating, you can also flavor it with candy oils. These intense flavorings are stronger than the regular flavorings and extracts you'll find in the baking section of the grocery store. You need to use only a small amount. Some flavor examples are blueberry, bubble gum, watermelon, and peppermint.

DIPPING METHODS

I mention these methods throughout the book, but they are so important that I want to provide them for you here in one place.

The question I have been asked the most is, "How do you get your coating so smooth?" Well, it's really simple.

Use small bowls so the melted candy coating is about 3 inches deep. Make sure the coating is thin enough to dip and remove the pops easily. You can use paramount crystals, shortening, or even vegetable oil to thin coatings. And then just tap excess coating off gently using one of the following methods.

CAKE BALLS: If you're making cake balls, drop a ball into a small, deep bowl of melted candy coating. Cover the entire ball with coating, using a spoon, without stirring or moving the cake ball around in the coating. Then lift it out of the coating with your spoon. With the ball still on the spoon, tap the handle of the spoon on the side of the bowl several times, until the excess coating starts to fall off and back into the bowl. Then let the cake ball slide off the spoon onto a wax paper–covered baking sheet to dry.

Complete instructions for cake balls start on page 11.

CAKE POPS: The same tapping technique works for cake pops, but it's done in a different way. Make sure your coating is deep enough to completely submerge the firmed cake pop. Small, narrow, and deep microwave-safe plastic bowls are best, so you can hold the bowl easily without burning any fingers. Glass bowls can get too hot. Dip about ½ inch of a lollipop stick into the melted coating and insert it into a cake ball, pushing it no more than halfway through.

Then dip the cake pop in the melted coating, completely covering the cake ball, and remove it in one motion. If the coating is too thick, gently tap off any excess. Hold the pop over the bowl in one hand and tap your wrist gently with your other hand. If you use the hand

holding the cake pop to shake off excess coating, the force of the movement will be too strong and could cause the cake ball to loosen or fly off the lollipop stick. Tapping the wrist holding the cake pop absorbs some of the impact. The excess coating will fall off, but you will need to rotate the lollipop stick so the coating doesn't build up on one side, making it too heavy on that side. If too much coating starts to build up at the base of the stick, simply use your finger to wipe it off, spinning the lollipop stick at the same time. This can happen if the coating is too thin or too hot. It's not as hard as it sounds; it just takes a little practice.

Complete instructions for cake pops start on page 15.

CUPCAKE POPS: This is a two-part dipping method, but it's actually the one I find the most fun to do. After you've formed the cupcake shapes with the cookie cutter and chilled them until firm, dip the bottom of a cupcake-shaped cake ball into the melted candy coating by holding the mounded top with your fingers. Dip to the point where the mounded cupcake top starts. Then turn your hand over to allow the coating to slide down. This will help make sure the entire cupcake bottom is covered in candy coating. While holding the shaped cupcake upside down, swirl your hand in a circular motion. This is equivalent to the tapping for the cake pops. The swirling motion forces the coating to slide down the side of the cupcake while creating a smooth surface at the same time. When the coating reaches the mounded top, transfer the cupcake pop to a wax paper–covered baking sheet, mounded-side down. Immediately insert a lollipop stick about ½ inch deep into the melted candy coating, and then insert the stick into the bottom of the cupcake no more than halfway through. Repeat with the remaining cupcake pops before you dip the tops.

When dipping the tops, let the second color of candy coating sit or cool for a few minutes before you start dipping. Coating that is too hot can run down the side. If it is slightly cool, it will stay in place.

To dip the top of a cupcake pop, hold the pop by the lollipop stick and dunk it into the melted candy coating until the top is completely covered and the coating meets the edge of the bottom candy coating. You can use a toothpick to direct the coating and touch up any exposed areas of cake.

Complete instructions for cupcake pops start on page 19.

CUPCAKE BITES: This is another two-part method. However, you dip only once. Place one type of melted candy coating in a squeeze bottle and use it to fill a cavity in a plastic candy cup mold about halfway. Place a firm cake ball (smaller in width than the mold shape) into the mold cavity. Slowly push the cake ball down until the pressure causes the candy coating to force its way up the mold and fill in around the sides of the cake ball. You may have to experiment with a couple to get the right amount of coating. Stop pushing once the coating reaches the top edge of the candy mold, so that it doesn't form a lip around the edge. Repeat for the remaining cavities. Place the mold in the freezer for several minutes to allow the coating to set. Remove the mold and pull out the cupcake bites by holding their exposed tops. Give the mold a little twist, too, to help release the cupcake bites.

Then simply dip the exposed mounded cupcake tops into a second melted candy coating by holding the cupcake bottoms. Try to be quick, because if you hold the bottom for too long, the ridges formed by the mold will pick up fingerprints. You can use candy gloves (see page 41) to help avoid this.

Complete instructions for cupcake bites start on page 25.

Dipping Do's & Don'ts

- DO use a bowl deep enough to dip your cake pops and remove them in one motion.

- DON'T get any water in your candy coating.

- DO keep a dry dish towel or paper towels nearby to wipe off your hands.

- DON'T overheat your candy coating.

- DO use shortening or paramount crystals to thin coating that is too thick.

- DON'T use regular food coloring to tint candy coating.

- DO use special candy coloring to tint it.

- DON'T push lollipop sticks more than halfway through the cake ball.

- DO dip the sticks in melted coating before you insert them into cake pops.

- DON'T dip frozen cake balls. Firm, yes. Frozen, no.

- DO have a lot of fun.

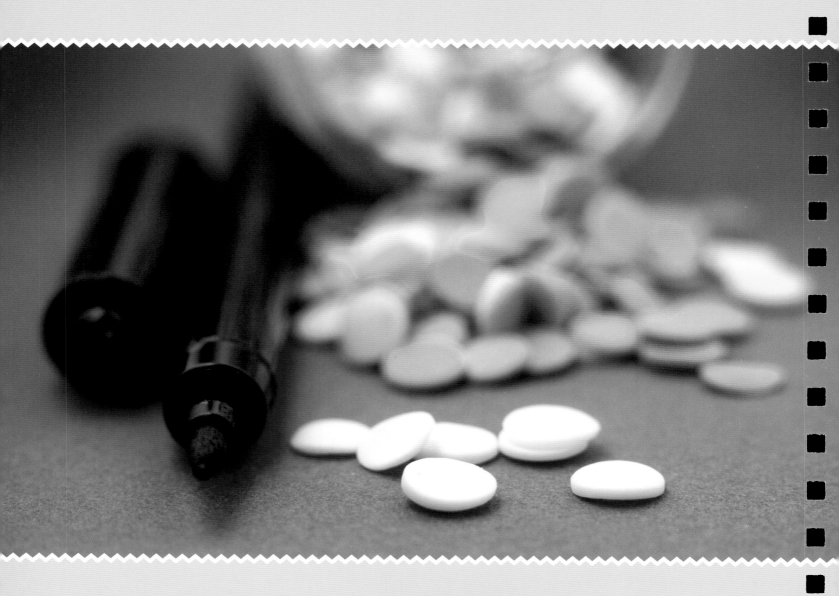

MY TWO FAVORITE TOOLS

Edible-Ink Pens

Dot your eyes. Edible-ink pens are an excellent tool to have on hand if you decide to add personality to your cake pops. They are quick and easy. Use them to draw eyes, mouths, eyelashes, and more. Americolor Gourmet Writer pens come in colors like black, brown, pink, red, blue, and more. You can buy a whole set or just black to suit your need.

Use them carefully. If you press down too hard when drawing on the candy coating, residue from the candy will build up on the tip, making the pens difficult to use. So use a very light touch. Imagine the pen as a paintbrush and the pops as your canvas. When dotting eyes on sprinkles, though, you'll need to press a little harder.

Toothpicks

Always keep a small container of toothpicks within reach.

You can use them to direct candy coating that may not have made its way completely around a cake pop. You can use it to texturize the surface of the candy coating. Or, if your candy coating pools at the bottom of the cake balls after they are placed on a wax paper–covered baking sheet to dry, simply take a toothpick and draw a line through the coating, close to the cake ball. When it dries, you can break off the unwanted coating for a cleaner look.

Toothpicks can also be used to apply candy coating as "glue." They are also extremely useful when adding decorations. After your cake pops are coated and dry, you can use any remaining candy coating left in your dipping bowl as glue. Apply it to candy or sprinkles with a toothpick and attach them to the cake pop. You can also apply the

candy coating to a coated, dry cake ball and then place the add-on into position. Use a tiny amount of coating to attach the smallest items, such as sprinkles for eyes. Use a slightly larger amount for bigger add-ons, such as M&M's or candy necklace pieces. When the coating dries, the add-on will be attached, or "glued" on. If the coating in the bowl has dried, simply heat it again to melt it.

MAIN INGREDIENTS

Here's a handy list of edible ingredients used in making cake pops.

CAKE: Cake mixes, homemade cakes, and store-bought cakes can all be used to create cake pops. Avoid using cakes that are extremely moist or that contain fruit, because when combined with frosting, the texture can become, for lack of a better word, gooey.

FROSTING: You can combine any flavor frosting with any flavor cake you like. Homemade frostings also work. If you're using frosting with perishable ingredients, such as cream cheese, make sure you store finished treats in the refrigerator. If you're using ready-made frosting, avoid the whipped varieties.

CANDY COATING: Coatings are widely available in disc form but are also available in blocks. Wilton and Make 'n Mold are popular brands that you can find in craft stores and even online. Merckens is another brand that is available online and in cake-supply stores. Grocery stores, such as Kroger, even carry their own brand of candy coating. Be aware that when ordering candy coating online during the summer months, your coating can arrive already melted. Don't worry, though; you can still use it.

CANDY COLORING: Wilton and Chefmaster are just two makers of candy coloring. These colorings are oil based and do not contain water. Never use regular food coloring, which does contain water, because it will ruin your candy coating.

CANDY WRITERS: Try these handy tubes of colored candy coating for smaller jobs. Just heat, following the directions on the package, and use right out of the tube. They're quick, easy, and definitely not messy. Colors include black, brown, red, white, yellow, green, orange, and pink, to name a few.

CANDY FLAVORING OILS: Use candy flavoring oils to add flavor to candy coatings. They are not a necessity by any means, but you may want to experiment for fun.

PARAMOUNT CRYSTALS: This product is ideal for thinning candy coating. It's available online from cake- and candy-supply Web sites and cake-supply stores. Shortening and even vegetable oil are also acceptable alternatives. Start by adding about a teaspoon per pound of coating until the coating is fluid enough for dipping.

EDIBLE ADD-ONS: Sprinkles, candies, nuts, and cookies are fun ways to transform plain cake pops into party pops for every occasion.

EDIBLE-INK PENS: Americolor Gourmet Writer is a popular brand of edible-ink pens. They come in packs of ten assorted colors, and a two-pack is also sold in black.

EQUIPMENT

You can make sensational treats with these simple tools. The following equipment is recommended for successful cake pops, cupcake pops, cake balls, and cupcake bites.

CAKE PAN: Use a 9-by-13-inch cake pan. Buy one with a lid—it will come in handy if you choose to bake the cake the night before you dip and decorate.

MIXER: You'll need to have one of these on hand, unless you use a store-bought cake and frosting.

MICROWAVE: I couldn't live without mine. You can melt candy coating colors as you need them if you have a microwave.

DOUBLE BOILER: Great for larger jobs, a double boiler can heat candy coating slowly, without letting the coating get too hot, but it is not a necessity.

COOKIE CUTTERS: Use a small flower-shaped cutter to make cupcake pops. Cutters should be about 1¼ inches wide by ¾ inch deep. Larger cutters 1½ inches wide by ½ inch deep can be used to make flowers and hearts. Round cutters can be used to cut candy melts into shapes for decorating.

MICROWAVE-SAFE BOWLS: Durable plastic bowls (not melamine) are ideal for melting candy coating in the microwave. They are light-weight and can be held without burning your hands while dipping. Look for bowls that are narrow and deep. Small bowls like this will make dipping much easier and will allow you to work with less coating at a time. Wide bowls will require you to melt more coating to make it deep enough for dipping. If the coating starts to get too low in the bowl to dip properly, you can transfer the coating to a coffee mug or smaller microwave-safe container. This will help you get the most out of your candy coating.

MIXING BOWLS AND SPOONS: Large mixing bowls and metal spoons are used to mix the cake and frosting together.

LOLLIPOP STICKS: Paper lollipop sticks are available in several different sizes and widths. I find the 6-inch length to be the most versatile for displaying.

STYROFOAM BLOCK: Use a block that's at least 2 inches thick, so the cake pops can be inserted far enough that they won't fall over. Poke holes about 2 inches apart in the top before you start dipping, so it will be ready when you need it. Do not poke the holes all the way through. A 12-by-18-inch block can hold 48 pops.

CANDY MOLDS: These are sold in hundreds of shapes and sizes The projects in this book use candy cup molds, square molds, disc-shaped molds, and more. Familiarize yourself with what's available and watch your creativity skyrocket.

BAKING SHEETS: Rimmed 12-by-18-inch baking sheets are large enough to hold 48 cake balls. However, smaller rimmed baking sheets are easy to slide in and out of the freezer or refrigerator—especially if you have a side-by-side model.

WAX PAPER: Keep wax paper handy for lining baking sheets before resting cake balls, cupcake pops, and cupcake bites on them; it allows them to be removed easily.

TOOTHPICKS: These are extremely useful for touch-ups, dipping, and decorating.

SMALL DISHES FOR SPRINKLES: Pour sprinkles into a small dish so you can pinch a few to sprinkle on each pop. Pouring them from the container can result in too much waste.

SQUEEZE BOTTLES: Perfect for drizzling and decorating, squeeze bottles come in small, medium, and large sizes to meet every need. You can also pour melted candy coating into resealable plastic bags. Just snip the corner off the bag and squeeze the coating through the hole.

DISH TOWELS: Always have a dish towel handy, especially when making cupcake pops. Coating can get on your fingers easily with this method, and it's better to wipe them on a dry dish towel than to risk getting water in your coating.

CANDY GLOVES: These are great if you are making cupcake bites. When holding the ridged cupcake bottoms formed by candy molds, your body heat can start to make impressions in the coating. Candy gloves can help prevent this. If you're a quick dipper, don't worry about having these around.

TWEEZERS: Keep a pair on hand for use solely in the kitchen. They can be helpful when attaching small add-ons to a cake-pop surface.

WARMING TRAY: This is a great tool to have around if you make a lot of cake pops and use more than one color, but it's not a necessity.

SPRINKLES

Sprinkles are so much fun. They come in tons of shapes, sizes, and colors. You'll be surprised by how easily they can be used to give cake pops pizzazz and personality. Here are some of the most commonly used sprinkles featured in this book. Keep in mind that in many cases, the single-color sprinkles used in these projects are separated from a container of multicolored sprinkles.

- Chocolate hearts mix
- Colorsticks
- Confetti sprinkles
- Halloween confetti sprinkles
- Jimmies (brown, orange, red)
- Jumbo confetti sprinkles (peach)
- Jumbo hearts (pink, red, white)
- Jumbo stars (yellow)
- Kissing lips
- Miniature hearts
- Multicolored diamonds
- Multicolored hearts
- Nonpareils
- Oval sprinkles
- Pastel sequins (also called miniature confetti sprinkles)
- Pastel wildflowers
- Poker shapes (black hearts)
- Rainbow chip sprinkles
- Sanding sugar
- Sugar pearls

Tip

- I like to buy seasonal sprinkles and keep them on hand. For instance, around Halloween you can find black sprinkles, which may be more difficult to find at other times of the year.

DECORATIVE ADD-ONS

Much like sprinkles, candy and other edible add-ons are fun to use for bringing life to your cake pops. Check out the candy aisle in your grocery store, drugstore, or even gas station. You'll start to see candy in a whole new way, inspiring your very own cake pop creations.

CANDIES

- Candy-coated sunflower seeds
- Candy necklace pieces
- Caramel candy corn
- Chocolate-coated espresso beans
- Dark chocolate–coated espresso beans
- French burnt peanuts
- Fruit Roll-Ups
- Hershey's Kisses
- Jelly beans
- Junior Mints
- Licorice belts
- Licorice buttons
- Licorice pastels
- Life Savers
- Life Savers Gummies
- M&M's
- M&M's Minis
- Pastel candy corn
- Rainbow Airheads Xtremes Sour Belts
- Red Hots
- Sour Punch Straws
- Tic Tacs
- Vanilla-coated espresso beans

FOOD ITEMS

- Alphabet pretzels
- Chocolate chips
- Coconut
- Japanese somen noodles
- Miniature marshmallows
- Mini Oreos
- Oreos
- Peanut butter chips
- Pretzel sticks
- Pretzel twists
- Sugar cones
- Teddy Grahams
- White chocolate chips

Sprinkles: 1. Seasonal Halloween confetti sprinkles 2. Pastel wildflowers 3. Rainbow chip sprinkles 4. Multicolored jumbo heart sprinkles 5. Kissing Lips 6. Orange and brown jimmies 7. Colorstick sprinkles 8. Jumbo heart sprinkles 9. Chocolate Hearts Mix 10. Jumbo star sprinkles 11. Jumbo diamond sprinkles 12. Sugar pearls 13. Miniature pink heart sprinkles. 14. Multicolored heart sprinkles 15. Easter egg sprinkles 16. Poker Shapes 17. Sanding sugars 18. Miniature confetti sprinkles 19. Confetti sprinkles 20. Jumbo confetti sprinkles.

Tip: Holidays are a great time to pick up specialty sprinkles. You can find colors and shapes that aren't available all year-round.

Candies: 1. Life Savers 2. Caramel candy corn 3. Pastel candy corn 4. Rainbow Airheads Xtremes Sour Belts 5. Life Saver Gummies 6. Licorice Bridge Mix (licorice buttons and pastels) 7. Jelly beans 8. Licorice Wheels 9. Tropical Chewy Lemonheads 10. Dark chocolate Hershey's Kisses 11. Tic Tacs 12. French burnt peanuts 13. Candy necklaces 14. Licorice pastels 15. Chocolate-coated and dark chocolate–coated espresso beans 16. M&M's 17. Gourmet Mints 18. Candy-coated sunflower seeds 19. Licorice belts 20. Seasonal Pink and Christmas M&M's 21. Sour Punch Straws 22. M&M's Minis

Tip: Around holidays, you can find candies like M&M's and candy corn in seasonal colors that aren't available other times of the year.

Food Items: 1. Chocolate chips 2. White chocolate chips 3. Miniature marshmallows 4. Oreos 5. Pecans 6. Butterscotch chips 7. Large chocolate chips 8. Teddy Grahams 9. Sugar Cones 10. Mini Oreos 11. Pretzel sticks 12. Coconut 13. Murray Sugar Free Chocolate Bites cookies

Tip

- The ingredient quantities on the following pages are based on making 48 cake pops. Keep in mind that you don't have to start off that big. Divide your cake into quarters, and use one quarter now and freeze the rest. Don't forget to reduce the amount of frosting and decorations proportionally. A dozen cake pops are plenty for the beginner and a great way to start without feeling overwhelmed.

Cake Pop *projects*

This section features dozens of ideas for decorating cake pops. From simple to show-stopping, they are some of the cutest treats on a stick. You'll be amazed at how easily sprinkles and candy pieces can transform average shapes into unique cake creations. Bunnies, monsters, flowers, clowns—there's no limit. The cake pops included here are just a starting point. I hope they inspire you to unleash your creativity and make something unique. You'll surprise yourself by what you are capable of. I know I did.

Whether you use a mix, bake from scratch, or purchase a store-bought cake to play with, these ideas are about having sweet fun. So grab some cake and frosting, pick up some candy coating and lollipop sticks, and let's get started.

Sweet Hearts

Nothing says Happy Valentine's Day better than sweetheart messages. Use a red edible-ink pen to express your love. Or maybe even just a "bite me" for fun.

YOU'LL NEED

48 uncoated Basic Cake Balls (page 11)

Metal heart-shaped cookie cutter, 1½ inches wide

16 ounces yellow candy coating

16 ounces pink candy coating

16 ounces light green candy coating

3 deep, microwave-safe plastic bowls

48 paper lollipop sticks

Styrofoam block

Red edible-ink pen

TO DECORATE

Remove the cake balls from the refrigerator and press them, one at a time, into a small heart-shaped cookie cutter to form the shape, or if you are adventurous, shape them by hand. They should be about 1½ inches wide and ½ inch deep.

After shaping, put the heart-shaped cakes in the freezer for about 15 minutes to firm them up again for dipping. Once they are firm, transfer them to the refrigerator. Remove a few at a time for dipping, keeping the rest chilled.

Melt each color of candy coating in a separate microwave-safe plastic bowl, following the instructions on the packages. The coating should be about 3 inches deep for easier dipping. Work with one color at a time before moving on to the next. (You should be able to get 16 heart-shaped cake pops from each pound of candy coating.)

One at a time, dip about ½ inch of the tip of a lollipop stick into the melted candy coating, and insert the stick straight into the bottom of a heart-shaped cake, pushing it no more than halfway through. Dip the cake pop into the melted coating, and tap off any excess coating, as described on page 36.

Let the pops dry in the Styrofoam block.

When they are completely dry, use a red edible-ink pen to write sweet notes on one side of each cake pop.

Return the pops to the Styrofoam block and let the ink dry completely.

Tip

- You can also use yellow M&M's or similarly shaped candy instead of gourmet mints for the flowers. However, the mints have a rounder surface similar to that of the licorice pastels.

Spring Fling

Butterfly- and flower-shaped cookie cutters provide an easy way to achieve distinctive shapes.

YOU'LL NEED

48 uncoated Basic Cake Balls (page 11)

Flower-shaped cookie cutter (1½ inches wide by ¾ inch deep)

Butterfly-shaped cookie cutter (1½ inches wide by ¾ inch deep)

48 ounces (3 pounds) white candy coating

Deep, microwave-safe plastic bowl

48 paper lollipop sticks

24 licorice pastels

24 yellow gourmet mints, or similar candy

Styrofoam block

Toothpicks

216 pastel confetti sprinkles (for flowers and butterflies)

48 jumbo heart sprinkles (for 24 butterflies)

48 rainbow colorstick sprinkles (for 24 butterflies)

TO DECORATE

Remove the cake balls from the refrigerator and mold half of the cake balls using a small flower-shaped cookie cutter and the other half using a small butterfly-shaped cookie cutter. Press the cake mixture into the cookie cutter until it fills up the shape.

After shaping, put the cake balls in the freezer for about 15 minutes to firm up again for dipping. Once they are firm, transfer them to the refrigerator.

Melt the white candy coating in a microwave-safe plastic bowl, following the instructions on the package. The coating should be about 3 inches deep for easier dipping. (I usually work with about 16 ounces of coating at a time.)

When you are ready to dip, remove a few shaped cake balls at a time from the refrigerator, keeping the rest chilled.

One at a time, dip about ½ inch of the tip of a lollipop stick into the melted candy coating, and insert the stick straight into the bottom of a butterfly- or flower-shaped cake ball, pushing it no more than halfway through. Dip the cake pop into the melted coating, and tap off any excess, as described on page 36. Before the coating sets, attach 1 licorice pastel to the front side of each butterfly and 1 yellow gourmet mint to the front of each flower. Let dry in the Styrofoam block.

For the flowers, use a toothpick to dot a small amount of melted coating to the fronts of the cake pops, so you can attach 1 confetti sprinkle on each flower petal.

For the butterflies, use a toothpick to dot a small amount of coating on the front of the cake pops so you can attach jumbo heart sprinkles and confetti sprinkles on each butterfly wing. Then insert 2 colorstick sprinkles in matching colors in the hardened coating on the top for antennae.

For an added detail, dot coating around the butterfly shape with a toothpick to define the wings.

Let dry completely in the Styrofoam block.

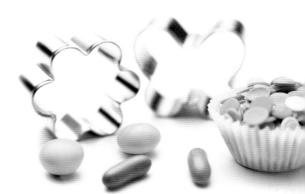

Spring Chicks

These adorable spring chicks are just the treat to add some pop to your Easter celebration.

YOU'LL NEED

48 uncoated Basic Cake Balls (page 11)

48 ounces (3 pounds) yellow candy coating

Deep, microwave-safe plastic bowl

48 paper lollipop sticks

Styrofoam block

Toothpicks

48 orange rainbow chip sprinkles

96 yellow rainbow chip sprinkles

96 orange wildflower sprinkles

Black edible-ink pen

Tip

- Try ditching the sticks. The chicks are pretty cute without them. Just form a cake ball into a pear shape and drop it into a bowl of melted candy coating. Cover it with the coating without moving or stirring it around in the bowl. Then lift it from the coating with a spoon using dipping instructions on page 36.

TO DECORATE

Have the cake balls chilled and in the refrigerator.

Melt the candy coating in a microwave-safe plastic bowl, following the instructions on the package. The coating should be about 3 inches deep for easier dipping. (I usually work with about 16 ounces of coating at a time.)

When you are ready to dip, remove a few cake balls at a time from the refrigerator, keeping the rest chilled.

One at a time, dip about ½ inch of the tip of a lollipop stick into the melted candy coating, and insert the stick straight into a cake ball, pushing it no more than halfway through. Dip the cake pop into the melted coating, and tap off any excess coating, as described on page 36.

Let dry completely in the Styrofoam block.

When the pops are dry, use a toothpick to dot a small amount of melted candy coating in position for the beak, and attach an orange rainbow chip sprinkle pointed-side out. Use the same technique to attach 2 yellow rainbow chips for wings, pointed-side out, on either side of the cake pop and 2 orange flower sprinkles at the bottom for feet.

Draw eyes with a black edible-ink pen, and let dry completely in the Styrofoam block.

Pastel Bunny Pops

YOU'LL NEED

48 uncoated Basic Cake Balls (page 11), formed into rounded triangular shapes

48 ounces (3 pounds) pink or white candy coating

Deep, microwave-safe plastic bowl

48 paper lollipop sticks

Styrofoam block

Round cookie cutter

96 pieces pastel candy corn

Toothpicks

48 pink jumbo heart sprinkles

96 white confetti sprinkles

Blue edible-ink pen

Black edible-ink pen

Pink edible-ink pen

TO DECORATE

Have the cake balls chilled and in the refrigerator.

Melt the candy coating in a microwave-safe plastic bowl, following the instructions on the package. The coating should be about 3 inches deep for easier dipping. (I usually work with about 16 ounces of coating at a time.)

When you are ready to dip, remove a few of the cake balls at a time from the refrigerator, keeping the rest chilled.

One at a time, dip about ½ inch of the tip of a lollipop stick into the melted candy coating, and insert the stick straight into the larger, bottom side of a shaped cake ball, pushing it no more than halfway through. Dip the cake pop into the melted coating, and tap off any excess coating, as described on page 36. Place in the Styrofoam block to dry.

For the ears, use a cookie cutter with a curved edge to cut off the tips of the candy corn. Dip the cut end of each candy corn piece in a little bit of the melted candy coating and attach it to the top of a bunny head. Hold the ears in place for a few seconds until the candy coating sets like glue, and place in the Styrofoam block to dry completely.

Use a toothpick to dot a small amount of melted candy coating in position for the nose, and attach 1 pink jumbo heart sprinkle. Hold it in place until set. Use the same technique to apply white confetti sprinkles for the eyes, and let dry.

Draw eye details on the confetti sprinkles with blue and black edible-ink pens. Draw the mouths with a pink edible-ink pen. Let the pops dry completely.

Tips

- When sprinkling the sugar pearls, work over a large bowl, because these tiny balls will bounce everywhere. You can also reuse the ones that fall into the bowl.

- You can also use soft edible pearls found in cake supply stores for an easier bite.

Sugar Sheep

Sugar pearls for wool make these sheep look so sweet. Be careful before you bite too hard, though. Sugar pearls are crunchy.

YOU'LL NEED

48 uncoated Basic Cake Balls (page 11), formed into oval shapes

48 ounces (3 pounds) white candy coating

Deep, microwave-safe plastic bowl

48 paper lollipop sticks

Styrofoam block

Licorice bridge mix (48 licorice buttons for heads and 96 licorice pastels cut in half for legs)

Sugar pearls

Toothpicks

48 tiny pink heart sprinkles

96 brown rainbow chip sprinkles

TO DECORATE

Have the cake balls chilled and in the refrigerator.

Melt the white candy coating in a microwave-safe plastic bowl, following the instructions on the package. The coating should be about 3 inches deep for easier dipping. (I usually work with about 16 ounces of coating at a time.)

When you are ready to dip, remove a few cake balls at a time from the refrigerator, keeping the rest chilled.

One at a time, dip about ½ inch of the tip of a lollipop stick into the melted candy coating, and insert the stick straight into the side of an oval cake ball, pushing it no more than halfway through. Dip the cake pop into the melted coating, and tap off any excess coating, as described on page 36.

Immediately attach 1 licorice button in position for the head and 4 pastel leg pieces by pushing them into the bottom, and sprinkle sugar pearls on the coating before it sets. If the coating is too hot, the attachments will slide off. If it has cooled for too long, the coating will set before you can finish attaching everything. But don't worry: if that happens, reheat the coating and use it as a glue to attach any remaining pieces. Let dry completely in the Styrofoam block.

For the face, use a toothpick to place tiny dots of melted white coating on the licorice-button heads for eyes. Using a toothpick, apply a dot of melted coating in position for the nose, and attach a tiny pink heart sprinkle. Use the same technique to apply brown rainbow chip sprinkles for ears.

Let dry completely in the Styrofoam block.

Confetti Easter Eggs

Dipping Easter eggs has never been so sweet. Coat egg-shaped cake balls in pastel-colored candy coating, and use corn syrup to attach colorful decorations.

YOU'LL NEED
48 uncoated Basic Cake Balls (page 11), formed into egg shapes

48 ounces (3 pounds) pink, white, or yellow candy coating

Deep, microwave-safe plastic bowl

48 paper lollipop sticks

Styrofoam block

Small paintbrush

Light corn syrup

Sanding sugar in various colors

Large bowl

Toothpicks

Pastel confetti sprinkles

TO DECORATE
Have the cake balls chilled and in the refrigerator.

Melt the candy coating in a microwave-safe plastic bowl, following the instructions on the package. The coating should be about 3 inches deep for easier dipping. (I usually work with about 16 ounces of coating at a time.)

When you are ready to dip, remove a few cake balls at a time from the refrigerator, keeping the rest chilled.

One at a time, dip about ½ inch of the tip of a lollipop stick into the melted candy coating, and insert the stick straight into the bottom of a shaped cake ball, pushing it no more than halfway through. Dip the cake pop into the melted coating, and tap off any excess coating, as described on page 36.

Let dry completely in the Styrofoam block.

When the pops are dry, use a small paintbrush to paint a thin layer of corn syrup in a line around an egg. Do one line at a time. Right after you paint on the syrup, sprinkle it with one of the sanding sugar colors until all the corn syrup is covered. Work over a large bowl, so you can catch and reuse the sugar.

Repeat, varying the designs and sanding sugar colors.

Use a toothpick to apply small dots of melted coating to the egg, and attach confetti sprinkles in random or uniform designs.

Let dry completely in the Styrofoam block.

Easter Baskets

Use jelly beans, coconut, and ice cream cones to decorate these Easter basket cake bites.

YOU'LL NEED

48 uncoated Basic Cake Balls (page 11)

14-ounce package sweetened flaked coconut

2 large resealable plastic bags

Pink and green pastel food coloring

48 sugar cones

Serrated knife

16 ounces peanut butter candy coating

2 deep, microwave-safe plastic bowls

Squeeze bottle

Disc-shaped plastic candy mold (with cavity openings 1⅜ inches wide)

Baking sheet

48 ounces (3 pounds) chocolate or vanilla candy coating

Spoon

48 green Sour Punch Straws

15-ounce bag jelly beans in assorted colors

TO DECORATE

Have the cake balls chilled and in the refrigerator.

Prepare the coconut the night before. Divide the coconut between the resealable plastic bags. Place a couple of drops of pink food coloring in one bag and add a little green coloring to the other. Close each bag and shake until the food coloring has been absorbed into the coconut. If you want the color to be darker, add another drop or two of food coloring to each bag. Let dry in the bag overnight.

For the baskets, cut off the bottoms of the sugar cones, using a serrated knife, so you are left with tops that are 1½ to 2 inches tall.

To complement the color of the sugar cones, melt the peanut butter candy coating in a microwave-safe bowl, following the instructions on the package, and pour it into a squeeze bottle.

Pipe the peanut butter candy coating into one cavity of the disc-shaped candy mold. Press a sugar cone into the cavity. The open bottom of the cone should fit snugly inside the disc to create the bottom of the basket. Repeat with the remaining cavities. Place the filled candy mold on a baking sheet for stability and put it in the freezer for a few minutes to let the coating set.

Remove from the freezer and lift the baskets from the mold by pulling gently on each sugar cone. Repeat to make the remaining sugar cone baskets.

Melt the chocolate or vanilla candy coating in a deep, microwave-safe plastic bowl. The coating should be about 3 inches deep for easier coating. (I usually work with about 16 ounces of coating at a time.)

(continued)

When you are ready to coat, remove a few cake balls at a time from the refrigerator, keeping the rest chilled.

One at a time, cover a cake ball with the melted chocolate or vanilla coating as described on page 36, and drop it into a basket with the spoon. You don't have to be concerned about a smooth finish, because these will be hidden from view by the coconut and cones.

For the handles, immediately insert each end of a Sour Punch Straw into the basket, on either side of the cake ball, before the coating sets. Once dry, the coating will help secure the basket handles in place.

Place some of the prepared colored coconut on top of each cake ball while the coating is still wet. Press slightly so the coconut is glued to the coating.

Use some of the coating to attach several jelly beans on top of the coconut for the eggs. Let dry completely.

Tips

- To speed things up, use more than one plastic disc mold.

- You can also use a squeeze bottle to add more coating before you sprinkle on the coconut. Make sure you pipe some where the straws are inserted, to help secure them.

- Decorate these the same day you want to serve them. The straws may break if they stay bent for too long.

- Save the sugar cone bottoms for the Ice Cream Cone Sundaes cake pops on page 67 or the Clowning Around cake pops on the facing page.

Clowning Around

Get creative with candy and decorate funny faces in an assortment of expressions.

YOU'LL NEED

48 uncoated Basic Cake Balls (page 11)

Serrated knife

48 or fewer sugar cones

48 ounces (3 pounds) white candy coating

Deep, microwave-safe plastic bowl

48 paper lollipop sticks

96 French burnt peanut candies

Styrofoam block

Toothpicks

48 red regular or peanut M&M's

Confetti colorstick sprinkles

Life Savers Gummies candies

Fruit Roll-Ups

Rainbow chip sprinkles

Black edible-ink pen

TO DECORATE

Have the cake balls chilled and in the refrigerator.

Prepare the clown hats first. Using a serrated knife, cut off about 1 inch of the tips of several sugar cones and set the tips aside; you won't need the tops of the cones. You don't have to do enough for all the cake pops. Some clowns can be hatless.

Melt the white candy coating in a microwave-safe plastic bowl, following the instructions on the package. The coating should be about 3 inches deep for easier dipping. (I usually work with about 16 ounces of coating at a time.)

When you are ready to dip, remove a few cake balls at a time from the refrigerator, keeping the rest chilled.

One at a time, dip about ½ inch of the tip of a lollipop stick into the melted candy coating, and insert the stick straight into a cake ball, pushing it no more than halfway through. Dip the cake pop into the melted coating, and tap off any excess coating, as described on page 36.

(continued)

Right after dipping each pop, gently attach 2 of the burnt peanut candies in position for the hair, and attach the sugar cone piece on top for the hat. Hold each in place for a few seconds, until the candy coating sets like glue. Place the pop in the Styrofoam block to dry. Repeat until you've used up the sugar cone "hats" and all of the clowns have hair.

For the face, use a toothpick to dot a small amount of melted candy coating in position for the nose and attach a red M&M. Hold it in place until set.

Using the same technique, attach 2 colorstick sprinkles for the eyebrows, using matching colors. Then add 1 Life Saver Gummies candy for the collar by sliding it up the lollipop stick and attaching it to the clown head with more melted candy coating. Try cutting out small sections from the candy for a more decorative effect before you attach it.

For the mouth, cut about a 1-inch rectangular piece of Fruit Roll-Up candy and roll it up tightly. Attach it, using more melted candy coating as glue.

Attach a colored rainbow chip sprinkle on the top of the sugar cone hat with candy coating.

Draw eyes with an edible-ink pen and let dry completely in the Styrofoam block.

Tips

- Switch things up. Don't make all the clowns alike. Some can go without hats and without collars. Some can have different-sized noses made of red peanut or regular M&M's. Attach the eyebrows and mouths at different angles for varied expressions.

- Reserve the tops of the sugar cones for the Easter Baskets on page 61, if you like.

Ice Cream Cone Sundaes

These miniature ice cream cone–cake pops will make a big impression.

YOU'LL NEED

48 uncoated Basic Cake Balls (page 11)

48 sugar cones

Serrated knife

Styrofoam block

Several lollipop sticks

48 ounces (3 pounds) pink candy coating

2 deep, microwave-safe plastic bowls

Multicolor sprinkles

16 ounces dark chocolate candy coating

Spoon

48 red peanut M&M's

TO DECORATE

Have the cake balls chilled and in the refrigerator.

Cut off the tops of the sugar cones, using a serrated knife, so that the width of the opening is about 1¼ inches.

Prepare your Styrofoam block. Since these have cone-shaped bottoms, you'll need to do more than just poke holes in the Styrofoam to support them. Take a lollipop stick, insert it at an angle, and then work it around in a circular motion until you have an opening in the Styrofoam that mimics the bottom shape of the cones.

Melt the pink candy coating in a microwave-safe plastic bowl, following the instructions on the package. The coating should be about 3 inches deep. (I usually work with about 16 ounces of coating at a time.)

When you are ready to coat, remove a few cake balls at a time from the refrigerator, keeping the rest chilled.

One at a time, cover a cake ball with the melted coating as described on page 36. Then insert a lollipop stick into the ball to lift it out. Transfer the coated cake ball to the prepared ice cream cone, and remove the stick. Don't worry about any excess coating or the hole left by the stick.

(continued)

The coated cake ball should rest nicely in the opening of the ice cream cone, and any excess coating will only enhance the look as it drips slightly down the edge. If the cake balls don't fit just right, make another cut in the cones so the opening is smaller, or make the cake balls bigger. Decorate with sprinkles while the pink candy coating is still wet.

Place the cones in the Styrofoam block to dry completely.

Melt the dark chocolate candy coating in the second microwave-safe plastic bowl. Spoon just a small amount over the very top of the ice cream cone. One at a time, attach a red peanut M&M on top before the chocolate coating sets, and return to the Styrofoam block to dry.

Tips

- You can reserve the unused sugar cone tops for the Easter Baskets project on page 61.

- For a variation, place a coated cake ball on wax paper, add sprinkles, and place the cone at an angle on top of the cake ball; it will look like a fun mistake.

Chocolate Cupcake Pops

Everyone loves a chocolate cupcake, but for even more fun add swirls to the top for a decorative touch. And don't stop at chocolate; these can be made using any candy coating color scheme.

YOU'LL NEED

48 uncoated Basic Cupcake Pops (page 19)

48 ounces (3 pounds) chocolate candy coating

2 deep, microwave-safe plastic bowls

Dish towel

Wax paper

2 baking sheets

48 paper lollipop sticks

Styrofoam block

Toothpicks

16 ounces white candy coating

Small squeeze bottle

TO DECORATE

Have the molded cupcake shapes chilled and in the refrigerator.

Melt the chocolate candy coating in a microwave-safe plastic bowl, following the instructions on the package. The coating should be about 3 inches deep for easier dipping. (I usually work with about 16 ounces of coating at a time.)

When you are ready to dip, remove a few cupcake shapes at a time from the refrigerator, keeping the rest chilled.

One at a time, take a shaped cupcake and, holding it by the mounded top, dip the bottom into the melted chocolate candy coating—just to the point where the mounded shape starts. Remove it from the chocolate, turn it upside down, and swirl your hand in a circular motion. This will cause any excess chocolate coating to slide down slightly. When the coating reaches the bottom of the mounded cupcake top shape, you can stop. Have a dish towel handy to wipe off your fingertips, as it is highly likely that you'll get some coating on them. Don't use water to rinse your hands, as getting water in the coating can make it unusable.

Place the half-coated cupcake shape on wax paper–covered baking sheets, with the candy-coated side up. Immediately dip about ½ inch of the tip of a lollipop stick into the chocolate candy coating, and insert the stick straight into the flat, chocolate-coated bottom of the cupcake while the coating is still wet. Push it no more than halfway through.

Continue with the rest of the cake balls and let dry completely in the Styrofoam block.

(continued)

Now you'll decorate the tops, resulting in a finished cupcake pop.

Holding its lollipop stick, dip the top of a cupcake in more of the melted chocolate candy coating. It should completely cover the rest of the exposed cupcake and meet the edge of the first chocolate coating.

Remove the cupcake pop from the coating, and turn it right-side up. If the chocolate is too hot, it will start to drip down the sides. If this happens, let the coating sit for a few minutes to thicken. Then when you dip the tops, the coating will stay in place. Use a toothpick to touch up any areas the melted chocolate didn't cover.

Let the pops stand in the Styrofoam block to dry completely.

Melt the white candy coating in the second plastic bowl, and pour it into the squeeze bottle. Pipe white swirls on the top of each cupcake pop for decoration and let dry.

Tips

• You can make these using pastel colors for a totally different look.

• You can dip the shaped cupcakes entirely in chocolate candy coating instead of using the two-step method; however, the cupcake tops will not be as defined.

Popcorn Bags

Turn any movie night into a sweet experience with these "popcorn" cake pops.

YOU'LL NEED

48 uncoated Basic Cake Balls (page 11)

48 ounces (3 pounds) white candy coating

Deep, microwave-safe plastic bowl

48 paper lollipop sticks

Styrofoam block

Small, sharp knife

144 miniature marshmallows

Black edible-ink pen

Red edible-ink pen

TO DECORATE

Remove the cake balls from the refrigerator and mold them into rectangular shapes to resemble popcorn bags.

After shaping, put the cakes in the freezer for about 15 minutes to firm them up for dipping. Once they are firm, transfer them to the refrigerator.

Melt the white candy coating in a microwave-safe plastic bowl, following the instructions on the package. The coating should be about 3 inches deep for easier dipping. (I usually work with about 16 ounces of coating at a time.)

When you are ready to dip, remove a few cake balls at a time from the refrigerator, keeping the rest chilled.

One at a time, dip ½ inch of the tip of a lollipop stick into the melted candy coating, and insert the stick straight into a rectangular cake ball, pushing it no more than halfway through.

Dip the cake pop into the melted coating, and tap off any excess coating, as described on page 36. Place in the Styrofoam block to dry.

Prepare the popcorn. Use a sharp knife to make 2 or 3 diagonal marks on each mini-marshmallow. Don't cut through the marshmallows.

When the cake pops are dry, dip the tops back in the melted candy coating. Hold them right-side up and attach 3 mini-marshmallows to each one. The marshmallows will attach more quickly if the candy coating is not too hot.

Repeat until all the cake pops have marshmallows attached, and let dry completely in the Styrofoam block.

Write "POP" on the front of each cake pop with a black edible-ink pen.

Draw vertical lines on each pop using a red edible-ink pen.

Return them to the Styrofoam block to let the ink dry completely.

Apple Pops

These are great little treats for teachers, for the first day of school or just for fun. You can make them plain or with sprinkles and edible-ink details for personality.

YOU'LL NEED

48 uncoated Basic Cake Balls (page 11)

Wax paper

Baking sheet

48 ounces (3 pounds) red candy coating

Deep, microwave-safe plastic bowl

48 paper lollipop sticks

24 pretzel sticks, broken into ½-inch pieces

48 green jumbo diamond sprinkles or similar green candy

Styrofoam block

Toothpicks

96 large white confetti sprinkles

Black edible-ink pen

TO DECORATE

Reshape the round cake balls so they are slightly wider at the top than the bottom. You can press down on the top and up on the bottom with your fingertips to make subtle indentations, creating an apple shape.

Place the apple-shaped cake balls on a wax paper–covered baking sheet and put in the freezer for about 15 minutes to firm them up for dipping. Once firm, transfer them to the refrigerator.

Melt the red candy coating in a microwave-safe plastic bowl, following the instructions on the package. The coating should be about 3 inches deep for easier dipping. (I usually work with about 16 ounces of coating at a time.)

When you are ready to dip, remove a few cake balls at a time from the refrigerator, keeping the rest chilled.

One at a time, dip about ½ inch of the tip of a lollipop stick into the melted candy coating, and insert the stick straight into the bottom of an apple-shaped cake ball, pushing it no more than halfway through. Dip the cake pop into the melted coating, and tap off any excess coating, as described on page 36.

While the coating is still wet, insert a pretzel piece on top for the stem, and attach 1 green jumbo sprinkle for the leaf. Place in the Styrofoam block to dry. Repeat until all the apple cake pops have the stems and leaves.

When the pops are dry, use a toothpick to dot a small amount of melted candy coating in position for the eyes, and attach 2 white confetti sprinkles. Place in the Styrofoam block to dry completely.

Draw on facial details, including pupils, eyelashes, and big smiles, using a black edible-ink pen.

Place in the Styrofoam block to dry.

Tip

• You can use a black edible-ink pen instead of sugar pearls to draw seed shapes on the strawberries once they are dry.

Strawberry Patch Pops

Pick these pops for any occasion and brighten someone's day.

YOU'LL NEED
48 uncoated Basic Cake Balls (page 11), formed into rounded triangular shapes

48 ounces (3 pounds) red candy coating

2 deep, microwave-safe plastic bowls

48 paper lollipop sticks

White sugar pearls

Styrofoam block

16 ounces dark green candy coating

Large squeeze bottle

Wax paper

Baking sheet

Toothpicks

Green Sour Punch Straws (optional)

TO DECORATE
Have the cake balls chilled and in the refrigerator.

Melt the red candy coating in a microwave-safe plastic bowl, following the instructions on the package. The coating should be about 3 inches deep for easier dipping. (I usually work with about 16 ounces of coating at a time.)

When you are ready to dip, remove a few of the cake balls at a time from the refrigerator, keeping the rest chilled.

One at a time, dip about ½ inch of the tip of a lollipop stick into the melted candy coating, and insert the stick straight into the bottom of each shaped cake ball, pushing it no more than halfway through. Dip the cake pop into the melted coating, and tap off any excess coating, as described on page 36.

Immediately place several sugar pearls onto the surface of the strawberries, and place the pops in the Styrofoam block to dry. Repeat until all the strawberries have been sprinkled with sugar pearls.

Melt the dark green candy coating in the second microwave-safe plastic bowl, and pour it into a large squeeze bottle. Pipe flower-like shapes with 5 rounded petals onto a wax paper-covered baking sheet for each of the 48 leaf tops. Fill in the shapes with more coating and let dry. You can place the baking sheet in the freezer to speed up the drying time. You can even make these the night before.

Reheat any leftover green coating and, with a toothpick, apply a small amount of coating to the top of the strawberry. One at a time, attach the leaf shapes, flat-side up, on top of the cake pops. Let dry in the Styrofoam block.

Optional: Cut the Sour Punch Straws up into 48 quarter-inch sections. Dip one end in some of the remaining green candy coating and attach in the center of each green-leaf top. Let dry completely.

Bride & Groom Cake Pops

These do-it-yourself wedding favors will impress any guest.

YOU'LL NEED

48 uncoated Basic Cake Balls (page 11)

64 to 80 ounces (4 to 5 pounds) white candy coating

Deep, microwave-safe plastic bowl

48 paper lollipop sticks

Styrofoam block

Wax paper

2 baking sheets

Large squeeze bottle

Black candy coloring (not food coloring)

Toothpicks

192 miniature white confetti sprinkles

48 miniature black heart sprinkles (from Poker Shapes)

TO DECORATE

Have the cake balls chilled and in the refrigerator.

Melt the white candy coating in a microwave-safe plastic bowl, following the instructions on the package. The coating should be about 3 inches deep for easier dipping. (I usually work with about 16 ounces of coating at a time.)

When you are ready to dip, remove a few cake balls at a time from the refrigerator, keeping the rest chilled.

One at a time, dip about ½ inch of the tip of a lollipop stick into the melted candy coating, and insert the stick straight into a cake ball, pushing it no more than halfway through. Dip the cake pop into the melted coating, and tap off any excess coating, as described on page 36.

For the grooms, place half of the cake pops in the Styrofoam block to dry; you will be dipping these a second time.

For the brides, place the remaining coated cake pops, ball-side down, on a wax paper–covered baking sheet, and let dry completely.

Transfer one-third of the remaining white candy coating to a large squeeze bottle, and pipe candy coating for the bride's dress in opposite directions (as shown in the photo). Place back on the wax paper to dry.

Tint the remaining two-thirds of the candy coating with black candy coloring. Keep adding color until you achieve a rich black. Then dip the groom cake pops in the black candy coating, holding the pop in a diagonal direction and dipping it into the coating until half covered. Remove and dip the other side in the opposite diagonal direction to form a black V-shaped jacket. Place the groom pops, ball-sides down, on a wax paper–covered baking sheet. Let the brides and grooms dry completely.

When the pops are dry, use a toothpick to dot a small amount of melted white candy coating in position for the bride's necklace and the groom's buttons, and attach white confetti sprinkles. Use the same technique to attach 2 black miniature heart sprinkles in position for the groom's bow tie. The pointed ends of the hearts should be facing each other when attached.

Use some of the leftover black candy coating to finish the bow ties. Just dip a toothpick into the coating and apply a small dab over the heart sprinkles where the two pointed sides meet. Let the brides and grooms dry completely.

Baby Faces

Throwing a baby shower? Share these baby-face cake pops with guests and they'll go gaga.

YOU'LL NEED

48 uncoated Basic Cake Balls (page 11)

4 to 8 ounces of pink candy coating

2 deep microwave-safe plastic bowls

2 small squeeze bottles

Wax paper

Baking sheet

48 ounces (3 pounds) white candy coating

48 paper lollipop sticks

Styrofoam block

Toothpicks

48 pastel candy necklace pieces

Black, pink, peach, and brown edible-ink pens

TO DECORATE

Have the cake balls chilled and in the refrigerator.

You can make the bows the night before. Melt the pink candy coating in a microwave-safe plastic bowl, following the instructions on the package. Pour into a small squeeze bottle. Pipe two small disks of the melted coating side by side on a wax paper–covered baking sheet. Then pipe one smaller disk in between, and overlapping, the other two for the bow. Decide how many girl babies you want to make, and repeat until you have that many bows. Let dry completely.

Melt the white candy coating in a microwave-safe plastic bowl, following the instructions on the package. The coating should be about 3 inches deep for easier dipping. (I usually work with about 16 ounces of coating at a time.)

When you are ready to dip, remove a few cake balls at a time from the refrigerator, keeping the rest chilled.

One at a time, dip about ½ inch of the tip of a lollipop stick into the melted white candy coating, and insert the stick straight into a cake ball, pushing it no more than halfway through. Dip the cake pop into the melted coating, and tap off any excess coating, as described on page 36.

For boy babies, place the pops in the Styrofoam block to dry.

For girl babies, attach 1 premade pink bow to the top of each head while the coating is still wet. Hold in place for a few seconds until the candy coating sets like glue, and place in the Styrofoam block to dry.

For the noses, pour the remaining white coating into the second squeeze bottle. Pipe small oval shapes onto wax paper and let dry. You can place them in the freezer on a baking sheet for a few minutes to speed this up.

When the pops are dry, use a toothpick to dot a small amount of melted candy coating in position for the nose, and attach a piped oval nose shape. Use the same technique to attach a candy necklace piece in position for the pacifier.

Use the edible-ink pens to draw on facial features, and let dry. Eyelashes, eyebrows, smiles, and blushing cheeks will give the pops personality.

Let dry completely.

Graduation Caps

In addition to making cupcake bites, you can use a candy cup mold to make other designs, such as these graduation caps. Try using candy coating in school colors and give your graduate even more to smile about.

YOU'LL NEED

48 uncoated Basic Cake Balls (page 11)

64 to 80 ounces (4 to 5 pounds) candy coating in the color of your choice

Deep, microwave-safe plastic bowl

Large squeeze bottle

Medium-sized plastic candy cup mold (with cavity openings 1½ inches wide)

48 paper lollipop sticks

Baking sheet

Styrofoam block

Shallow square plastic candy mold (with cavity openings 1⅞ inches wide)

Toothpicks

Rainbow Airheads Xtremes Sour Belts, separated into colors and cut into 2-inch pieces

M&M's Minis or similarly shaped candy for the cupcake tops

TO DECORATE

Have the cake balls chilled and in the refrigerator. Refer to the Basic Cupcake Bites method on page 25 when making these graduation caps.

Melt the candy coating in a microwave-safe bowl, following the package directions, and pour into a large squeeze bottle.

Fill a cavity of the candy cup mold with melted coating, and place a cake ball into the opening. Press it in slowly, allowing the candy coating to force its way up the sides of the candy mold. The top of the ball should be flush with the top surface of the plastic mold. In other words, it should not stick up past the top of the candy mold cavity. If the balls are too large, simply pinch off a little bit and roll them smaller. You can also shape them similar to the shape of the mold cavity to maximize space.

Use the squeeze bottle to pour more candy coating over the top of the cake ball. The coating should be level with the surface of the plastic mold. Immediately insert a lollipop stick into the cake ball, pushing it no more than halfway through. Repeat with the remaining cavities and let dry. You can place the filled candy mold on a baking sheet in the freezer to speed up the drying time. Remove after 5 to 10 minutes, and pop them out by pressing on the mold underneath. Using chilled cake balls here helps the sticks stand up straight when you insert them, but to be safe, don't try to pull them out by the sticks when they are dry.

(continued)

Repeat, using the same candy mold, or use several molds at once. Stand the pops in the Styrofoam block.

Make the tops for the hats, using a shallow square candy mold. Fill each square with melted candy coating. Hold the tray above the counter surface and gently drop it a couple of times to flatten the coating. Place the tray on a baking sheet in the freezer to speed up the drying time. Remove after about 5 minutes, pop the squares out of the mold, and set aside.

When all the hat pieces are completed and dry, you can do the final assembly. Using a toothpick, place some candy coating on the bottom of each square hat piece and attach the pieces to the cake pop to complete the shape. Using the same gluing technique, apply a small amount of coating to the top of the hat and attach a Sour Belt candy tassel and 1 M&M's Mini in the center.

Let dry completely in the Styrofoam block.

Tip

- Pull-apart licorice pieces are another option for the tassel if you can't find Rainbow Sour Belts.

Pool Party Pops

These fun cupcake pops are perfect for a pool party or beach theme.

YOU'LL NEED

48 uncoated Basic Cupcake Pops (page 19)

Pink candy writer

Yellow candy writer

48 Teddy Grahams cookies

Black edible-ink pen

48 Life Savers Gummies candies

48 ounces (3 pounds) light blue candy coating

Deep, microwave-safe plastic bowl

Wax paper

Baking sheet

48 paper lollipop sticks

Styrofoam block

Toothpicks

Blue sanding sugar

TO DECORATE

Have the molded cupcake shapes chilled and in the refrigerator.

Prepare the bathing suits on the bears first. Use candy writers to pipe pink bikinis onto Teddy Grahams for girl bears and yellow candy swim trunks for boy bears. Let dry. Use a black edible-ink pen to detail the faces.

Stretch Life Savers Gummies, place them around the legs of the teddy bears, and set aside.

Melt the blue candy coating in a microwave-safe plastic bowl, following the instructions on the package. The coating should be about 3 inches deep for easier dipping. (I usually work with about 16 ounces of coating at a time.)

When you are ready to dip, remove a few cupcake shapes at a time from the refrigerator, keeping the rest chilled.

One at a time, take a cupcake shape and, holding it by its mounded top, dip the bottom into the melted candy coating. Remove it from the candy coating, turn it upside down, and swirl your hand in a circular motion. This will cause any excess coating to slide down slightly. When the coating reaches the bottom of the mounded shape, you can stop.

Place the half-coated cupcake shape on a wax paper–covered baking sheet, with the candy-coated side up. Immediately dip about ½ inch of the tip of a lollipop stick into the melted candy coating, and insert the stick straight into the flat, candy-coated bottom of the cupcake while the coating is still wet. Push it no more than halfway through.

(continued)

Continue with the rest of the cupcake shapes and let dry completely.

Now you'll decorate the tops, resulting in a finished cupcake pop.

One at a time, hold the lollipop stick and dip the top of the cupcake into the melted blue candy coating. It should completely cover the rest of the exposed cake ball and meet the edge of the first coating.

Remove the cupcake pop from the coating, and turn it right-side up. If the coating is too hot, it will start to drip down the sides. If this happens, just let the coating sit for a few minutes to thicken. Then when you dip the tops, the coating will stay in place.

Use a toothpick to touch up any areas the melted candy coating didn't cover and to create wavy lines in the coating.

While the coating is still wet, sprinkle the top of the cupcake pop with blue sanding sugar and attach one of the teddy bears. The Life Saver inner tube should rest on top. Let dry completely in the Styrofoaı

Tip

- You can also dip the shaped cupcakes entirely in blue candy coating instead of using the two-step method; however, the cupcake tops will not be as well defined.

Martians

Dark green and pink candy coating make these mini-Martians out-of-this-world cute! Add black sunflower-seed eyes to create spooky space invaders.

YOU'LL NEED
48 uncoated Basic Cake Balls (page 11), formed into balloon shapes

24 ounces (1½ pounds) dark green candy coating

2 deep, microwave-safe plastic bowls

48 paper lollipop sticks

Styrofoam block

24 ounces (1½ pounds) dark pink candy coating

Toothpicks

96 black candy-coated sunflower seeds

TO DECORATE
Have the cake balls chilled and in the refrigerator.

Melt the dark green candy coating in a microwave-safe plastic bowl, following the instructions on the package. The coating should be about 3 inches deep for easier dipping. (I usually work with about 16 ounces of coating at a time.)

When you are ready to dip, remove a few cake balls at a time from the refrigerator, keeping the rest chilled.

One at a time, dip about ½ inch of the tip of a lollipop stick into the melted candy coating, and insert the stick straight into the pointed end of a shaped cake ball, pushing it no more than halfway through. Dip the cake pop into the melted coating, and tap off any excess coating, as described on page 36. Do this with half of the cake balls, and place them in the Styrofoam block to dry.

Melt the dark pink candy coating in the second bowl, and dip the remaining Martians, adding them to the Styrofoam block.

When the pops dry, use a toothpick to dot a small amount of candy coating (matching the color of the pop) in position for the eyes. Attach 2 coated sunflower seeds, pointed sides facing in and down. Hold them in place until the candy coating sets like glue.

Place the pops back in the Styrofoam block to dry completely.

Tip

- If you don't have a microwave-safe bowl large enough for
  3 pounds of candy coating, you can work in batches, melting
  more coating as you need it. Keep in mind that the shade
  of gray may not match from one batch to another.

Robots

Candy necklace pieces make great eyes, especially for these colorful robots. Place them close together or far apart, and have fun with their faces.

YOU'LL NEED

48 uncoated Basic Cake Balls (page 11), formed into squares and/or rectangles

48 ounces (3 pounds) white candy coating

Deep, microwave-safe plastic bowl

Black candy coloring (not food coloring)

48 paper lollipop sticks

Styrofoam block

Toothpicks

96 candy buttons

Candy necklace pieces in assorted colors (you'll need at least 144)

Red Rips Licorice Belts

Life Savers Candies

Japanese somen noodles

TO DECORATE

Have the cake shapes chilled and in the refrigerator.

Melt the white candy coating in a microwave-safe plastic bowl, following the instructions on the package. The coating should be about 3 inches deep for easier dipping. Stir a few drops of black candy color into the melted white coating until you achieve the desired shade of gray.

When you are ready to dip, remove a few cake balls at a time from the refrigerator, keeping the rest chilled.

One at a time, dip about ½ inch of the tip of a lollipop stick into the melted candy coating, and insert the stick straight into a cake ball, pushing it no more than halfway through. Dip the cake pop into the melted coating, and tap off any excess coating, as described on page 36.

Let dry in the Styrofoam block.

To attach the robot details, use a toothpick to dot a small amount of melted gray candy coating in position for the ears and attach 2 candy buttons that match in color. Place 2 dots of coating in position for the eyes and attach matching candy necklace pieces. Cut mouths out of the Red Rips Licorice Belts, and attach them in position using the same technique. The coating will dry and work like glue.

Using a toothpick again, apply coating at the base of the robot head where it meets the stick, and attach a Life Saver by sliding it up the lollipop stick. Hold it in place until the candy coating sets like glue. Add more coating to the bottom of the Life Saver and attach a candy necklace piece in the same way.

Break the somen noodles into ½-inch pieces, and carefully insert them into the tops of the cake pops for antennae. Some robots can have one antenna and some can have two. For robots with one antenna, you can attach another candy necklace piece around the antenna, using the same gluing technique.

Have fun and create an assortment of expressions by varying the placement of the candy pieces.

Let dry completely in the Styrofoam block.

Monster Pops

Kids will get a kick out of these cake pops. Let them help and make messy monsters.

YOU'LL NEED

48 uncoated Basic Cake Balls (page 11)

64 ounces (4 pounds) purple candy coating

Deep, microwave-safe plastic bowl

48 paper lollipop sticks

Styrofoam block

Large squeeze bottle

White candy writer

Chocolate jimmies

Blue edible-ink pen

Black edible-ink pen

TO DECORATE

Have the cake balls chilled and in the refrigerator.

Melt the purple candy coating in a microwave-safe plastic bowl, following the instructions on the package. The coating should be about 3 inches deep for easier dipping. (I usually work with about 16 ounces of coating at a time.)

When you are ready to dip, remove a few cake balls at a time from the refrigerator, keeping the rest chilled.

One at a time, dip about ½ inch of the tip of a lollipop stick in the melted candy coating, and insert the stick straight into a cake ball, pushing it no more than halfway through. Dip the cake pop into the melted coating, and tap off any excess coating, as described on page 36.

Let dry in the Styrofoam block.

Pour the remaining purple coating into a large squeeze bottle, and pipe random, drizzled lines all around the monster head. Let dry completely in the Styrofoam block.

On some of the pops, pipe two small white circles with a candy writer for the eyes, and insert 2 chocolate jimmies before the coating sets.

On the remaining pops, pipe a single large, white circle. Let dry completely and draw a large blue circle inside the white circle, using a blue edible-ink pen. With a black edible-ink pen, outline the circle and draw a pupil to finish the eye.

Let dry completely.

note: You can also use melted white candy coating for the eyes.

Pirate Pops

Watch out! These double-dipped pirate pops will steal your heart with their friendly faces.

YOU'LL NEED

48 uncoated Basic Cake Balls (page 11)

48 ounces (3 pounds) white candy coating

2 deep, microwave-safe plastic bowls

48 paper lollipop sticks

Styrofoam block

24 ounces red candy coating

About 15 white confetti sprinkles per cake pop

Toothpicks

48 red M&M's Minis

48 red jumbo heart sprinkles

Black edible-ink pen

TO DECORATE

Have the cake balls chilled and in the refrigerator.

Melt the white candy coating in a microwave-safe plastic bowl, following the instructions on the package. The coating should be about 3 inches deep for easier dipping. (I usually work with about 16 ounces of coating at a time.)

When you are ready to dip, remove a few cake balls at a time from the refrigerator, keeping the rest chilled.

One at a time, dip about ½ inch of the tip of a lollipop stick into the melted white candy coating, and insert the stick straight into a cake ball, pushing it no more than halfway through. Dip the cake pop into the white coating, and tap off any excess coating, as described on page 36.

Let dry completely in the Styrofoam block.

For the bandanas, melt the red candy coating in the second microwave-safe plastic bowl and dip the top half of each cake pop in it, holding the pop at a diagonal. Before the red candy coating sets, place miniature white confetti sprinkles randomly on top. (You can also attach the sprinkles after the coating dries by using a toothpick to dot on coating and then attaching the sprinkles.)

Let dry completely in the Styrofoam block.

To finish the bandanas, use a toothpick to dab a little red candy coating onto one side of the pop, and attach a red M&M's Mini. Hold it in place until the candy coating sets like glue. Use the same technique to attach a jumbo heart sprinkle, with the pointed end toward the cake pop, for the final touch, and let dry.

For the faces, use a black edible-ink pen to draw on eyes, patches, and mouths.

Let dry completely.

Game Ball Cupcake Bites

Use a candy mold to make cupcake bites, and decorate these sweet treats for your favorite sport.

YOU'LL NEED

48 uncoated Basic Cupcake Bites (page 25)

48 ounces (3 pounds) chocolate candy coating

2 or more deep, microwave-safe plastic bowls

Large squeeze bottle

Medium-sized plastic candy cup mold (with cavity openings 1½ inches wide)

Baking sheet

24 ounces (1½ pounds) white, yellow, or orange candy coating

Toothpicks

White candy writer, for tennis balls

Small squeeze bottle

Red candy writer or candy coating, for baseballs

Red jimmies, for baseballs

Black candy writer, for soccer balls and basketballs

Tip

- The ridges formed in the chocolate by the candy mold can melt slightly when you hold them for more than a few seconds. Wearing candy gloves can reduce fingerprints on the coating.

TO DECORATE

Have the cake balls chilled and in the refrigerator. Refer to the Basic Cupcake Bites method on page 25 when making these Game Ball Bites.

Melt the chocolate candy coating in a microwave-safe plastic bowl, following the package instructions, and transfer it to a large plastic squeeze bottle.

Use the large squeeze bottle to fill a cavity of the candy mold with chocolate coating, and immediately place one of the cake balls into the coating. Start out by filling the cavity about halfway. Slowly push the cake ball down until the pressure causes the candy coating to force its way up and fill in around the sides of the cake ball. You may have to experiment with a couple to get the right amount. Stop pushing once the chocolate reaches the top edge of the candy mold so that it doesn't form a lip around the edge. Half of the uncoated cake ball should be raised above the mold to form a mounded top. Repeat with the remaining cavities of the mold.

Place the filled candy mold tray in the freezer for 5 to 10 minutes to allow the chocolate to set. Placing it on a baking sheet will keep the candy mold from bending.

Remove from the freezer and separate the cupcake bites from the candy mold. Give the mold a twist and pull, holding on to the exposed cake balls.

For the soccer and baseball cupcake tops, melt the white candy coating in a microwave-safe bowl. For the tennis balls, melt the yellow candy coating, and for basketballs, melt the orange candy coating.

(continued)

Holding the bottom of each cupcake bite, dip the top in the melted candy coating until it meets the edge of the chocolate coating. You can use a toothpick to touch up any uncoated areas.

Remove the cupcake bite from the coating, turn it right-side up, and swirl your hand in a circular motion to help smooth out the coating. Set aside and let dry completely before decorating the details.

For tennis balls, use a white candy writer (or pour some melted white coating into the small squeeze bottle) and pipe on wavy seams.

For baseballs, use a red candy writer (or melted red candy coating) to pipe semicircles onto the tops. Add red jimmies while the coating is still wet, or pipe on red for the stitches, and let dry.

For soccer balls, use a toothpick to etch hexagon shapes into the white coated tops. You can use the markings as a guide to outline the shapes using a black candy writer. Fill the shapes in with black.

For basketballs, use a toothpick to etch two perpendicular lines and then two semicircles. Trace the markings with a black candy writer.

Let the cupcake bites dry completely.

In addition to cake balls, bites, and pops, you can combine other ingredients that will allow you to mold different shapes. These footballs are actually crushed Oreos mixed with cream cheese. You can shape them out of cake and frosting as well, but don't limit yourself. Feel free to experiment with other sweets, like cookies, and brownies. Or for other pop examples, visit: www.bakerella.com/category/pops-bites/other-pops/

Lovely Little Ladybugs

Create cute bug bites using domed candy molds.

YOU'LL NEED

48 uncoated Basic Cake Balls (page 11)

64 ounces (4 pounds) red candy coating

2 deep, microwave-safe plastic bowls

Large squeeze bottle

Dome-shaped plastic truffle candy mold (with cavity openings 1¾ inches wide)

Baking sheet

Black edible-ink pen

4 ounces of chocolate candy coating

Toothpicks

48 Junior Mints

96 white confetti sprinkles

48 red lip-shaped sprinkles

About 400 black confetti sprinkles

96 chocolate jimmies

TO DECORATE

Have the cake balls chilled and in the refrigerator. Refer to the Basic Cupcake Bites method on page 25 when making these ladybug bites.

Melt the red candy coating in a microwave-safe bowl, following the package directions, and pour into a large squeeze bottle.

Fill a cavity of the domed candy mold with the melted red coating, and place a cake ball into the cavity. Press it in slowly, allowing the candy coating to force its way up the sides of the candy mold. The top of the ball should be almost flush with the top of the plastic mold. In other words, it should not stick up past the top of the candy mold cavity. If the balls are too large, simply pinch off a little bit and roll them smaller. You can also shape them similar to the shape of the mold cavity to maximize space.

(continued)

Use the squeeze bottle to pour more red candy coating over the top of the cake ball. The coating should be level with the surface of the plastic mold. Repeat with each cavity and let dry. You can place the filled mold on a baking sheet in the freezer to speed this up. Remove after 5 to 10 minutes, and pop the red ladybug bodies out of the mold. Repeat using the same candy mold, or use several molds at once.

Draw a straight black line down the center of each domed, candy-covered cake ball with a black edible-ink pen and let dry.

Work on the heads next. Melt the chocolate coating to use as glue. Use a toothpick to dot melted chocolate candy coating onto each Junior Mint in position for the eyes, and attach 2 white confetti sprinkles. Use the same technique to attach 1 red lip sprinkle in position for the mouth. Set aside to dry.

Using a toothpick, dot more chocolate coating onto either side of the line on the ladybug's back. Press 1 black confetti sprinkle on each dot of coating and let dry.

Place a small amount of chocolate coating on the back of each Junior Mint head and attach to the ladybug body. Allow to dry completely before moving. Finally, dip a toothpick into the melted chocolate coating and dot on the pupils of the eyes. Dip the ends of 2 chocolate jimmies, one at a time, in melted chocolate coating and attach in place on each head for the antennae.

Optional: If you would like the ladybugs to have feet, attach 2 black confetti sprinkles to the underside of the ladybug body with more candy coating, so that half of the confetti sprinkle is exposed for view. Allow to dry completely before moving.

Tips

- The antennae and feet will be very delicate, so be careful. If you plan on presenting these at home, they should do fine, but if you want to transport them, consider skipping the feet and antennae.

- You can also pipe on spots with candy coating instead of using black confetti sprinkles.

Froggies

Use white candy necklace pieces for eyes that pop, and draw on a big smile to round out these happy faces.

YOU'LL NEED

48 uncoated Basic Cake Balls (page 11)

48 ounces (3 pounds) dark green candy coating

Deep, microwave-safe plastic bowl

48 paper lollipop sticks

96 white candy necklace pieces

Styrofoam block

Black edible-ink pen

1 package (5.64 ounces) Red Rips Licorice Belts (optional)

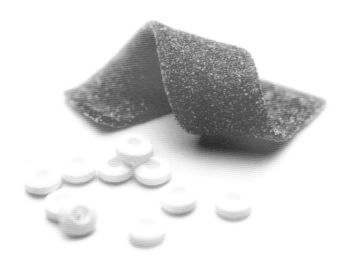

TO DECORATE

Have the cake balls chilled and in the refrigerator.

Melt the dark green candy coating in a microwave-safe plastic bowl, following the instructions on the package. The coating should be about 3 inches deep for easier dipping. (I usually work with about 16 ounces of coating at a time.)

When you are ready to dip, remove a few cake balls at a time from the refrigerator, keeping the rest chilled.

One at a time, dip about ½ inch of the tip of a lollipop stick into the melted candy coating, and insert the stick straight into a cake ball, pushing it no more than halfway through. Dip the cake pop into the melted coating, and tap off any excess coating, as described on page 36.

While the coating is still wet, attach 2 candy necklace pieces in position for the eyes, and place in the Styrofoam block to dry. Repeat until all the froggie cake pops have eyes.

Draw a nose and a big smile with a black edible-ink pen, and let dry completely in the Styrofoam block.

Optional: Cut tongue shapes from the licorice belts. They should be round on one end for the tip of the tongue and slightly curved on the other to attach more easily to the curved surface of the cake pop. Dip the slightly curved end in melted candy coating and attach it along the frog's smile. Hold it in place for a few seconds until the candy coating sets like glue, and let dry.

Barnyard Friends

Pink Piggies

Make these little piggies, as well as cow and chicken pops, for a barnyard birthday bash.

YOU'LL NEED

48 uncoated Basic Cake Balls (page 11)

48 ounces (3 pounds) pink candy coating

Deep microwave-safe plastic bowl

48 paper lollipop sticks

96 pink candy-coated sunflower seeds

Styrofoam block

Toothpicks

48 light pink M&M's

Red edible-ink pen

Black edible-ink pen

TO DECORATE

Have the cake balls chilled and in the refrigerator.

Melt the pink candy coating in a microwave-safe plastic bowl, following the instructions on the package. The coating should be about 3 inches deep for easier dipping. (I usually work with about 16 ounces of coating at a time.)

When you are ready to dip, remove a few cake balls at a time from the refrigerator, keeping the rest chilled.

One at a time, dip about ½ inch of the tip of a lollipop stick into the melted candy coating, and insert the stick straight into a cake ball, pushing it no more than halfway through. Dip the cake pop into the melted coating, and tap off any excess coating, as described on page 36.

While the coating is still wet, gently attach 2 candy-coated sunflower seeds in position for the ears.

Place in the Styrofoam block to dry. Repeat until all the cake pops are dipped and have ears.

When the pops are dry, use a toothpick to dot a small amount of melted candy coating in position for the nose, and attach 1 pink M&M, M-side down. Hold in place for a few seconds, until set.

Place in the Styrofoam block to dry completely. Repeat until all the cake pops have noses.

Draw details, using a red edible-ink pen for the snout and a black edible-ink pen for the eyes and mouth.

Let dry completely.

(continued)

Cow Pops

Chocolate chips are the perfect proportion for many animal ears. Here you can use one in white chocolate and one in milk chocolate for adorable little cows.

YOU'LL NEED

48 uncoated Basic Cake Balls (page 11)

48 ounces (3 pounds) white candy coating

Deep, microwave-safe plastic bowl

48 paper lollipop sticks

Styrofoam block

Toothpicks

48 light pink M&M's

48 white chocolate chips

48 milk chocolate chips

Brown or black candy writers

96 white miniature confetti sprinkles

Black edible-ink pen

TO DECORATE

Have the cake balls chilled and in the refrigerator.

Melt the white candy coating in a microwave-safe plastic bowl, following the instructions on the package. The coating should be about 3 inches deep for easier dipping. (I usually work with about 16 ounces of coating at a time.)

When you are ready to dip, remove a few cake balls at a time from the refrigerator, keeping the rest chilled.

One at a time, dip about ½ inch of the tip of a lollipop stick into the melted candy coating, and insert the stick straight into a cake ball, pushing it no more than halfway through. Dip the cake pop into the melted coating, and tap off any excess coating, as described on page 36. Place in the Styrofoam block to dry.

For the face, use a toothpick to apply a small amount of melted coating on the front of the pop, in position for the nose, and attach 1 pink M&M, M-side down. Hold it in place until set.

Use the same technique to attach a white and milk chocolate chip to each pop for the ears.

Place in the Styrofoam block to dry completely.

Use a candy writer to pipe a small circle of coating onto each pop for a cow spot. Use a toothpick to dot on some candy coating, and attach 1 miniature confetti sprinkle eye inside the spot and another sprinkle on the other side for the eyes.

Using a black edible-ink pen, draw pupils on the confetti sprinkles, snout details, and a mouth. Let dry completely.

Chickens

Heart sprinkles come in different sizes. See how easily miniature and jumbo-size hearts turn plain white cake pops into super-cute chicks.

YOU'LL NEED

48 uncoated Basic Cake Balls (page 11)

48 ounces (3 pounds) white candy coating

Deep, microwave-safe plastic bowl

48 paper lollipop sticks

144 red jumbo heart sprinkles

Styrofoam block

Toothpicks

96 orange miniature heart sprinkles

Black edible-ink pen

TO DECORATE

Have the cake balls chilled and in the refrigerator.

Melt the white candy coating in a microwave-safe plastic bowl, following the instructions on the package. The coating should be about 3 inches deep for easier dipping. (I usually work with about 16 ounces of coating at a time.)

When you are ready to dip, remove a few cake balls at a time from the refrigerator, keeping the rest chilled.

One at a time, dip about ½ inch of the tip of a lollipop stick into the melted candy coating, and insert the stick straight into a cake ball, pushing it no more than halfway through. Dip the cake pop into the melted coating, and tap off any excess coating, as described on page 36.

Immediately attach the pointed side of 3 red jumbo heart sprinkles in a line on the top of the cake pop. Place in the Styrofoam block to dry. Repeat with the remaining cake pops until all the chicken pops have red jumbo sprinkles on top.

When the pops are dry, use a toothpick to dot a small amount of melted candy coating in position for the beak, and attach 2 miniature orange heart sprinkles, pointed-side out. Separate them slightly so that the beak looks open. Hold them in place until the candy coating sets like glue, and place in the Styrofoam block to dry.

Draw eyes with a black edible-ink pen. Let dry completely.

⟳ Puppy Pops

Mix and match peanut butter, chocolate, and vanilla candy coatings to create a litter of cute puppies.

YOU'LL NEED

48 uncoated Basic Cake Balls (page 11)

32 ounces (2 pounds) peanut butter candy coating

16 ounces white candy coating

2 deep, microwave-safe plastic bowls

48 paper lollipop sticks

Styrofoam block

16 ounces chocolate candy coating

1 to 3 squeeze bottles

Several large clear plastic spoons

Permanent marker

Wax paper

Baking sheet

M&M's Minis

Small, sharp knife

Toothpicks

Black edible-ink pen

48 Life Savers candies

TO DECORATE

Have the cake balls chilled and in the refrigerator.

Melt the peanut butter and white candy coatings in separate plastic microwave-safe bowls, following the instructions on the packages and working with one flavor at a time. The coating should be about 3 inches deep for easier dipping.

When you are ready to dip, remove a few cake balls at a time from the refrigerator, keeping the rest chilled.

One at a time, dip about ½ inch of the tip of a lollipop stick in either melted candy coating, and insert the stick straight into a cake ball, pushing it no more than halfway through. Dip the cake pop into the same melted coating, and tap off any excess coating, as described on page 36.

Let the pops dry in the Styrofoam block.

To make the puppy ears, melt the chocolate candy coating and pour in a squeeze bottle. If you want ears in the other colors, put some of the peanut butter and white candy coatings into separate squeeze bottles, reheating them if necessary.

Draw an elongated teardrop shape on the back of a large plastic spoon with a permanent marker. Using plastic spoons will help you form ears that are curved. Turn the spoon over. Using a squeeze bottle filled with melted coating, trace the ear shape on the inside bowl of the spoon, then fill the shape with more coating. Repeat until you have 48 pairs of puppy ears. Place in the freezer on a wax paper–covered baking sheet for a few minutes to set.

(continued)

Remove the spoons from the freezer and simply pop the ears off them. Store in a safe place until you are ready to attach them to the cake pops. These can even be made the night before.

For the noses, cut M&M's Minis in half, using a sharp knife. You can also use a squeeze bottle filled with melted candy coating to pipe noses onto wax paper. Let the noses dry completely. These can be made the night before too.

Use a toothpick to dot a small amount of melted candy coating in position for the nose and attach a candy nose or a nose made of coating.

Let the pops dry completely in the Styrofoam block.

Draw eyes and a mouth on each puppy with an edible-ink pen, and let dry completely.

Attach the ears and Life Savers for the collars with more melted candy coating, sliding the Life Savers onto the lollipop sticks. Hold each in place for a few seconds until the candy coating sets like glue.

Let dry completely.

note: The ears will be fragile. Be extremely careful if transporting.

Lions, Tigers & Bears, Oh My!

Little Lions

Make these lion cake pops using peanut butter morsels and they'll be the "mane" attraction.

YOU'LL NEED

48 uncoated Basic Cake Balls (page 11)

48 ounces (3 pounds) peanut butter or butterscotch candy coating

Deep, microwave-safe plastic bowl

48 paper lollipop sticks

Styrofoam block

24 brown M&M's

Sharp knife

11-ounce package peanut butter or butterscotch morsels

Toothpicks

96 miniature white confetti sprinkles

Black edible-ink pen

TO DECORATE

Have the cake balls chilled and in the refrigerator.

Melt the candy coating in a microwave-safe plastic bowl, following the instructions on the package. The coating should be about 3 inches deep for easier dipping. (I usually work with about 16 ounces of coating at a time.)

When you are ready to dip, remove a few cake balls at a time from the refrigerator, keeping the rest chilled.

One at a time, dip about ½ inch of the tip of a lollipop stick into the melted candy coating, and insert the stick straight into a cake ball, pushing it no more than halfway through. Dip the cake pop into the melted coating, and tap off any excess coating, as described on page 36.

Place in the Styrofoam block to dry and repeat with the remaining cake pops.

Cut the M&M's in half with a sharp knife and set aside.

Dip the bottom of a peanut butter morsel into the leftover melted candy coating and attach it to the cake pop. Continue all the way around the head, using about a dozen morsels, to create the mane. Let the pops dry in the Styrofoam block.

When the pops are dry, use a toothpick to dot a small amount of melted candy coating in position for the nose, and attach an M&M half. Use the same technique to attach 2 miniature white confetti sprinkles for the eyes. Repeat with the remaining cake pops and let dry.

Draw on the mouths and pupils for the eyes with a black edible-ink pen.

Place in the Styrofoam block to dry.

(continued)

Tiny Tigers

Use a black edible-ink pen to transform orange cake pops into terrific-looking tigers.

YOU'LL NEED
48 uncoated Basic Cake Balls (page 11)

48 ounces (3 pounds) orange candy coating

Deep, microwave-safe plastic bowl

48 paper lollipop sticks

Styrofoam block

48 orange candy necklace pieces

Sharp knife

Toothpicks

48 miniature black heart sprinkles (from Poker Shapes)

96 miniature white confetti sprinkles

White candy writer

Black edible-ink pen

TO DECORATE
Have the cake balls chilled and in the refrigerator.

Melt the orange candy coating in a microwave-safe plastic bowl, following the instructions on the package. The coating should be about 3 inches deep for easier dipping. (I usually work with about 16 ounces of coating at a time.)

When you are ready to dip, remove a few cake balls at a time from the refrigerator, keeping the rest chilled.

One at a time, dip about ½ inch of the tip of a lollipop stick into the melted candy coating, and insert the stick straight into a cake ball, pushing it no more than halfway through. Dip the cake pop into the melted coating, and tap off any excess coating, as described on page 36.

Place in the Styrofoam block to dry.

Cut the orange candy necklace pieces in half, using a sharp knife.

Dip the cut side of 2 candy necklace pieces into the leftover melted coating, and attach them to a cake pop for the ears. Hold them in place until the coating sets like glue. Repeat for the remaining cake pops.

Let dry in the Styrofoam block.

When the pops are dry, use a toothpick to dot a small amount of melted candy coating in position for the nose, and attach a miniature black heart sprinkle. Use the same technique to attach 2 miniature white confetti sprinkles in position for the eyes.

Use a white candy writer to pipe two small circle patches on either side of the tiger's nose, and let dry.

Draw on the tiger stripes and pupils for the eyes with a black edible-ink pen.

Let dry completely.

(continued)

Brown Bears

These bears are made using chocolate candy coating, but you can make them in any color you want. Pink or blue bears would make cute baby shower treats.

YOU'LL NEED

48 uncoated Basic Cake Balls (page 11)

48 ounces (3 pounds) chocolate candy coating

Deep, microwave-safe bowl

48 paper lollipop sticks

Styrofoam block

48 dark brown or black M&M's

Sharp knife

Toothpicks

48 miniature black heart sprinkles (from Poker Shapes)

96 miniature white confetti sprinkles

Black edible-ink pen

TO DECORATE

Have the cake balls chilled and in the refrigerator.

Melt the candy coating in a microwave-safe plastic bowl, following the instructions on the package. The coating should be about 3 inches deep for easier dipping. (I usually work with about 16 ounces of coating at a time.)

When you are ready to dip, remove a few cake balls at a time from the refrigerator, keeping the rest chilled.

One at a time, dip about ½ inch of the tip of a lollipop stick into the melted candy coating, and insert the stick straight into a cake ball, pushing it no more than halfway through. Dip the cake pop into the melted coating, and tap off any excess coating, as described on page 36.

Place in the Styrofoam block to dry and repeat with the remaining cake pops.

Cut the M&M's in half with a sharp knife and set side.

Dip the flat side of 2 M&M's pieces into the melted coating and attach them to the cake pop for ears. Hold them in place until the coating sets like glue. Repeat for the remaining cake pops.

Let dry in Styrofoam block.

When the pops are dry, use a toothpick to dot a small amount of melted candy coating in position for the nose, and attach a miniature black heart sprinkle. Use the same technique to attach 2 miniature white confetti sprinkles in position for the eyes.

Draw on the mouths and pupils for the eyes with a black edible-ink pen.

Place in the Styrofoam block to dry.

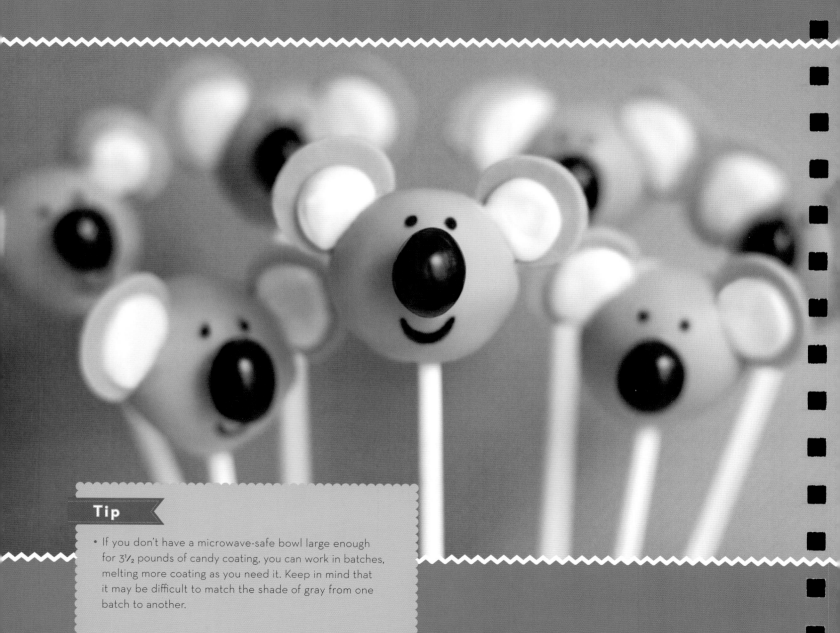

Tip

- If you don't have a microwave-safe bowl large enough for 3½ pounds of candy coating, you can work in batches, melting more coating as you need it. Keep in mind that it may be difficult to match the shade of gray from one batch to another.

Koala Bears

Candy coating comes in a rainbow of colors. You can also tint your own easily. For gray, add a few drops of black candy coloring to melted white candy coating.

YOU'LL NEED
48 uncoated Basic Cake Balls (page 11),

64 ounces (4 pounds) white candy coating

2 deep, microwave-safe plastic bowls

Black candy coloring (not food coloring)

48 paper lollipop sticks

Styrofoam block

2 large squeeze bottles

Wax paper

Round metal cookie cutter

Toothpicks

48 dark chocolate–coated espresso beans

Black edible-ink pen

TO DECORATE
Have the cake balls chilled and in the refrigerator.

Melt 56 ounces (3½ pounds) white candy coating in a microwave-safe plastic bowl, following the instructions on the package. The coating should be about 3 inches deep for easier dipping.

Add several drops of black candy coloring to the melted white coating and stir, adding more, a drop at a time, if necessary until you achieve the desired shade of gray.

When you are ready to dip, remove a few cake balls at a time from the refrigerator, keeping the rest chilled.

One at a time, dip about ½ inch of the tip of a lollipop stick into the melted candy coating, and insert the stick straight into a cake ball, pushing it no more than halfway through. Dip the cake pop into the melted coating, and tap off any excess coating, as described on page 36.

Let the pops dry in the Styrofoam block.

Now work on the ears. Pour the unused gray candy coating into a large squeeze bottle. You can reheat it if necessary.

For each koala bear cake pop, pipe two 1¼-inch round discs on wax paper for the ears. Let dry completely.

Use any cookie cutter with a slightly rounded edge to cut away a curved shape from the ear. The curved cut should be similar in shape to the side of the cake pop, so you can attach the two without a gap.

To attach the ears, use a toothpick to apply a small amount of melted gray candy coating on the side of the ear where the cut was made. Attach each ear to the pop, flat-side forward, and place the pop back in the Styrofoam block to dry. The coating will dry and work like glue. Repeat until all the cake pops have gray ears.

Melt the remaining 8 ounces of white candy coating and pour it into a large squeeze bottle. Carefully pipe round white circular shapes on the flat surface of the attached gray ears while holding the lollipop stick, making sure a gray border is exposed around the edges, and let dry. If the white coating drips, it is too hot. Let the coating sit for a minute to thicken, and continue.

For the face, use a toothpick to apply a small amount of melted gray coating to the front of the pop in position for the nose, and attach an espresso bean. Hold it in place for a few seconds, until the candy coating sets like glue.

Draw eyes and a mouth with an edible-ink pen and let dry completely in the Styrofoam block.

Panda Bears

These little bears are black and white and cute all over.

YOU'LL NEED

48 uncoated Basic Cake Balls (page 11)

96 black M&M's

Small, sharp knife

48 ounces (3 pounds) white candy coating

Deep, microwave-safe plastic bowl

48 paper lollipop sticks

Styrofoam block

Toothpicks

48 miniature black heart sprinkles (from Poker Shapes)

Black candy writer

96 miniature white confetti sprinkles

Black edible-ink pen

Pink heart sprinkles, blue heart sprinkles, and blue confetti sprinkles (optional)

TO DECORATE

Have the cake balls chilled and in the refrigerator.

Prepare the panda ears. Cut off a third of each M&M with a sharp knife and use the remaining two-thirds for the ears. Set aside.

Melt the white candy coating in a microwave-safe plastic bowl, following the instructions on the package. The coating should be about 3 inches deep for easier dipping. (I usually work with about 16 ounces of coating at a time.)

When you are ready to dip, remove a few cake balls at a time from the refrigerator, keeping the rest chilled.

One at a time, dip about ½ inch of the tip of a lollipop stick into the melted candy coating, and insert the stick straight into a cake ball, pushing it no more than halfway through. Dip the cake pop into the melted coating, and tap off any excess coating, as described on page 36.

While the coating is still wet, attach 2 of the M&M's pieces in position for the ears. Hold in place for a few seconds until the candy coating sets like glue, and place in the Styrofoam block to dry.

When the pops are dry, use a toothpick to dot a small amount of melted candy coating in position for the nose, and attach 1 black miniature heart sprinkle.

Use a black candy writer to pipe coating on either side of the nose, in position for the eyes. Attach 2 miniature white confetti sprinkles before the coating sets. Let dry completely.

Use the black edible-ink pen to draw on the mouth and pupils for the eyes.

Place in the Styrofoam block to dry.

Optional: To make girl pandas, use a pink heart sprinkle for the nose. You can also make a bow using 2 blue heart sprinkles, attached with the pointed ends facing each other, and 1 blue confetti sprinkle overlapping the center. Attach each piece by using a toothpick to apply melted candy coating as glue.

Monkey Business

Use peanut butter morsels and candy coating wafers to decorate these monkey cake pops. Make them with chocolate cake and frosting and you won't be sorry.

YOU'LL NEED

48 uncoated Basic Cake Balls (page 11)

48 ounces (3 pounds) chocolate candy coating

Deep, microwave-safe plastic bowl

48 paper lollipop sticks

96 peanut butter morsels

96 peach jumbo confetti sprinkles

Styrofoam block

Toothpicks

96 black confetti sprinkles

48 peanut butter candy coating wafers

48 brown rainbow chip sprinkles

Black edible-ink pen

TO DECORATE

Have the cake balls chilled and in the refrigerator.

Melt the chocolate candy coating in a microwave-safe plastic bowl, following the instructions on the package. The coating should be about 3 inches deep for easier dipping. (I usually work with about 16 ounces of coating at a time.)

When you are ready to dip, remove a few cake balls at a time from the refrigerator, keeping the rest chilled.

One at a time, dip about ½ inch of the tip of a lollipop stick into the melted candy coating, and insert the stick straight into a cake ball, pushing it no more than halfway through. Dip the cake pop into the melted coating, and tap off any excess coating, as described on page 36.

While the coating is still wet, attach the pointed side of 2 peanut butter morsels in position for the eyes, and insert 2 peach jumbo confetti sprinkles on each side of the cake pop for the ears. Let dry completely in the Styrofoam block.

When the pops are dry, use a toothpick to dot a small amount of melted candy coating on each peanut butter morsel, and attach 2 black confetti sprinkles to finish the eyes.

Apply melted candy coating to the back of a peanut butter candy coating wafer and place it on the pop, slightly overlapping the bottom of the peanut butter morsel eyes, to create the mouth area. Hold it in place until the coating sets like glue.

Place in the Styrofoam block to dry and repeat with the remaining pops.

When the pops are dry, use a toothpick to dot a small amount of melted candy coating in position for the nose and attach 1 brown rainbow chip sprinkle.

Draw a big smile with a black edible-ink pen across the width of the peanut butter coating wafer, and let dry completely.

Tips

- If you don't have a microwave-safe bowl large enough for 3 pounds of candy coating, you can work in batches, melting more coating as you need it. Keep in mind that the shade of black may not match from one batch to another.

- To create ears that are more subtle in appearance, attach them to the cake pop before you dip. Just add a little coating to the bottom of each morsel and attach them in position for the ears. Let dry in the Styrofoam block, and then dip the entire cake pop, with ears attached. See the Owls on page 132 for an example.

Black Cats

Use black candy coloring to make these cake pops "purr"-fect for Halloween.

YOU'LL NEED

48 uncoated Basic Cake Balls (page 11)

48 ounces (3 pounds) white candy coating

Deep, microwave-safe plastic bowl

Black candy coloring (not food coloring)

48 paper lollipop sticks

Styrofoam block

96 chocolate chips

Kitchen knife

Toothpicks

48 red rainbow chip sprinkles

96 yellow or white oval sprinkles

Black edible-ink pen

TO DECORATE

Have the cake balls chilled and in the refrigerator.

Melt the white candy coating in a microwave-safe plastic bowl, following the instructions on the package. The coating should be about 3 inches deep for easier dipping. (I usually work with about 16 ounces of coating at a time.)

Tint the coating with black candy coloring. Keep adding color, stirring, until the coating is dark enough.

When you are ready to dip, remove a few cake balls at a time from the refrigerator, keeping the rest chilled.

One at a time, dip about ½ inch of the tip of a lollipop stick into the melted candy coating, and insert the stick straight into a cake ball, pushing it no more than halfway through. Dip the cake pop into the melted coating, and tap off any excess coating, as described on page 36.

Let dry in the Styrofoam block.

Now work on the ears. Submerge the chocolate chips in the black candy coating, one at a time. Remove (you can use the end of a kitchen knife to lift them out) and attach 2 to the top of each pop for the ears. Hold them in place until the candy coating sets like glue, and place in the Styrofoam block to dry. Repeat until all the cake pops have black ears.

When the pops are dry, use a toothpick to dot a small amount of melted candy coating in position for the nose, and attach a red rainbow chip sprinkle. Use the same technique to attach 2 oval sprinkles for the eyes.

Using a black edible-ink pen, draw a straight line down the center of each oval sprinkle to finish the eyes. Let dry completely.

note: You can also use round confetti sprinkles for the eyes.

Jack-o'-Lanterns

Trick or treat. Here's something cute to eat.

YOU'LL NEED

48 uncoated Basic Cake Balls (page 11)

48 ounces (3 pounds) orange candy coating

Deep, microwave-safe plastic bowl

48 paper lollipop sticks

48 green Tic Tac mints or similarly shaped candy

Styrofoam block

Black edible-ink pen

TO DECORATE

Have the cake balls chilled and in the refrigerator.

Melt the orange candy coating in a microwave-safe plastic bowl, following the instructions on the package. The coating should be about 3 inches deep for easier dipping. (I usually work with about 16 ounces of coating at a time.)

When you are ready to dip, remove a few cake balls at a time from the refrigerator, keeping the rest chilled.

One at a time, dip about ½ inch of the tip of a lollipop stick into the melted candy coating, and insert the stick straight into a cake ball, pushing it no more than halfway through. Dip the cake pop into the melted coating, and tap off any excess coating, as described on page 36.

Immediately insert a Tic Tac on the very top of the pumpkin pop. Hold in place until set, and let dry completely in the Styrofoam block. Repeat with the remaining pumpkins until they all have stems.

Draw on jack-o'-lantern faces with a black edible-ink pen, and let dry completely in the Styrofoam block.

Ghostly Goodies

Draw surprised, scary, or just plain silly faces on these ghosts for a giggle.

YOU'LL NEED

48 uncoated Basic Cake Balls (page 11), formed into bell shapes

48 ounces (3 pounds) white candy coating

Deep, microwave-safe plastic bowl

48 paper lollipop sticks

Styrofoam block

Black edible-ink pen

TO DECORATE

Have the cake balls chilled and in the refrigerator.

Melt the white candy coating in a microwave-safe plastic bowl, following the instructions on the package. The coating should be about 3 inches deep for easier dipping. (I usually work with about 16 ounces of coating at a time.)

When you are ready to dip, remove a few shaped cake balls at a time from the refrigerator, keeping the rest chilled.

One at a time, dip about ½ inch of the tip of a lollipop stick into the melted candy coating, and insert the stick straight into the bottom of a shaped cake ball, pushing it no more than halfway through. Dip the cake pop into the melted coating, and tap off any excess coating, as described on page 36.

Place in the Styrofoam block to dry.

Draw eyes and a mouth with a black edible-ink pen, and let dry completely in the Styrofoam block.

Tip

- You can easily transform these into skulls. Just reshape the rolled cake balls into skull shapes. Visualize a light bulb as you hand-form the shapes. Then just draw on skull faces with a black edible-ink pen.

Tip

- The hats are delicate and may not do well if you will be transporting or wrapping the pops. These would be better served at a home Halloween gathering.

Spooky Witches

Cookies and candies create cute hats to top off these Halloween treats.

YOU'LL NEED

48 uncoated Basic Cake Balls (page 11), formed into oval shapes

24 Oreos

Table knife

48 ounces (3 pounds) dark green candy coating

Deep, microwave-safe plastic bowl

48 paper lollipop sticks

48 green Tic Tac mints

Licorice wheels, cut into 192 pieces, each 1½ inches long

Styrofoam block

Toothpicks

96 orange jimmies

48 Hershey's Kisses Brand Special Dark Chocolates

Black edible-ink pen

TO DECORATE

Have the oval cake balls chilled and in the refrigerator.

Separate the Oreos, scraping off the cream center with a table knife, so that you have 48 hat pieces; set aside.

Melt the dark green candy coating in a microwave-safe plastic bowl, following the instructions on the package. The coating should be about 3 inches deep for easier dipping. (I usually work with about 16 ounces of coating at a time.)

When you are ready to dip, remove a few shaped cake balls at a time from the refrigerator, keeping the rest chilled.

One at a time, dip about ½ inch of the tip of a lollipop stick in the melted candy coating, and insert the stick straight into the bottom of a shaped cake ball, pushing it no more than halfway through. Dip the cake pop into the melted coating, and tap off any excess coating, as described on page 36.

Before the coating sets, attach a Tic Tac in position for the nose and an Oreo cookie half on top for the hat. Attach two 1½-inch licorice wheel sections on either side of the witch's head for hair. Hold them in place until the candy coating sets like glue, and Place in the Styrofoam block to dry. You can add more coating on the sides to attach the pieces if the coating sets too fast.

When the pops are dry, use a toothpick to dot a small amount of melted candy coating in position for the eyes, and attach 2 orange jimmies on each cake pop.

To finish the hats, tear off the paper sticking out of each Hershey's Kiss, and use a toothpick to apply a small amount of coating on the center of the Oreo hat bottom. Attach the wrapped chocolate candy in place and let dry.

Draw mouths with a black edible-ink pen, and let dry completely in the Styrofoam block.

Yummy Mummies

Use a squeeze bottle to pipe on white candy coating for easy mummy faces.

YOU'LL NEED

48 uncoated Basic Cake Balls (page 11), formed into oval shapes

64 ounces (4 pounds) white candy coating

Deep, microwave-safe plastic bowl

48 paper lollipop sticks

Styrofoam block

Large squeeze bottle

Green candy writer

TO DECORATE

Have the cake balls chilled and in the refrigerator.

Melt the white candy coating in a microwave-safe plastic bowl, following the instructions on the package. The coating should be about 3 inches deep for easier dipping. (I usually work with about 16 ounces of coating at a time.)

When you are ready to dip, remove a few cake balls at a time from the refrigerator, keeping the rest chilled.

One at a time, dip about ½ inch of the tip of a lollipop stick into the melted candy coating, and insert the stick straight into the bottom of a shaped cake ball, pushing it no more than halfway through. Dip the cake pop into the melted coating, and tap off any excess coating, as described on page 36.

Let dry completely in the Styrofoam block.

Pour the remaining melted white coating into a large squeeze bottle and pipe lines across the front of each mummy face. Let dry completely in the Styrofoam block.

Use a green candy writer to pipe two dots on the front of each cake pop for the eyes.

Let dry completely.

Owls

These cake pops are a hoot with their big eyes and sprinkle feet.

YOU'LL NEED

48 uncoated Basic Cake Balls (page 11), formed into rounded triangular shapes

48 ounces (3 pounds) chocolate candy coating

Deep, microwave-safe plastic bowl

48 paper lollipop sticks

96 chocolate chips

Styrofoam block

Toothpicks

96 white candy necklace pieces

48 orange rainbow chip sprinkles

96 small pink flower sprinkles

96 brown M&M's Minis

TO DECORATE

Have the cake balls chilled and in the refrigerator.

Melt the chocolate candy coating in a microwave-safe plastic bowl, following the instructions on the package. The coating should be about 3 inches deep for easier dipping. (I usually work with about 16 ounces at a time.)

When you are ready to dip, remove a few cake balls at a time from the refrigerator, keeping the rest chilled.

One at a time, dip about ½ inch of the tip of a lollipop stick into the melted candy coating, and insert the stick straight into the pointed tip of the triangular cake ball, pushing it no more than half-way through. Dip the bottoms of 2 chocolate chips into the melted candy coating, and attach them to the front top of the head for "ears." Place in the Styrofoam block to dry.

Dip the cake pops into the melted candy coating, as described on page 36. Make sure the coating is deep enough so you can get the entire cake pop, with ears attached, submerged in one dunk. Remove and gently tap off any excess coating.

Place in the Styrofoam block to dry.

When the pops are dry, use a toothpick to dot a small amount of melted candy coating in position for the eyes and attach 2 white candy necklace pieces.

Using the same technique, dot candy coating in position for the beak, and attach an orange rainbow chip sprinkle. Then attach 2 pink flower sprinkles for the feet and 2 brown M&M's Minis for the wings.

Let dry completely in the Styrofoam block.

Turkey Time

Serve these on Thanksgiving Day and your guests will gobble them right up.

YOU'LL NEED

48 uncoated Basic Cake Balls (page 11)

48 ounces (3 pounds) chocolate candy coating

Deep, microwave-safe plastic bowl

48 paper lollipop sticks

48 pretzel sticks, broken in half

Styrofoam block

240 caramel candy corn pieces (14 ounces)

Toothpicks

48 candy-coated espresso beans, in shades of brown

48 orange rainbow chip sprinkles

48 red miniature heart sprinkles

Black edible-ink pen

TO DECORATE

Have the cake balls chilled and in the refrigerator.

Melt the chocolate candy coating in a microwave-safe plastic bowl, following the instructions on the package. The coating should be about 3 inches deep for easier dipping. (I usually work with about 16 ounces of coating at a time.)

When you are ready to dip, remove a few cake balls at a time from the refrigerator, keeping the rest chilled.

One at a time, dip about ½ inch of the tip of a lollipop stick into the melted candy coating, and insert the stick straight into a cake ball, pushing it no more than halfway through. Dip the cake pop into the melted candy coating, and tap off any excess coating, as described on page 36.

Immediately insert the tips of 2 pretzel stick halves into the bottom of the turkey body, on either side of the lollipop stick, for legs. Hold them in place until the coating sets like glue. Repeat until all the cake pops have legs. Let dry completely in the Styrofoam block.

Dip the tips of 5 pieces of candy corn into the leftover melted candy coating, and attach them to the back of a cake pop for feathers. Hold them in place until the coating sets like glue. Repeat until all the cake pops have feathers. Let dry completely in the Styrofoam block.

Using a toothpick, apply a small amount of coating to the front and toward the top of the cake pop, and attach an espresso bean. Hold in place until the coating sets. Repeat with the remaining pops and let dry completely.

When the pops are dry, use a toothpick to dot a small amount of coating onto the espresso bean in position for the beak, and attach an orange rainbow chip sprinkle. Use the same technique to attach a red miniature heart sprinkle upside down under the beak for the wattle. Repeat with the remaining pops and let dry completely in the Styrofoam block.

Draw eyes on the espresso beans with a black edible-ink pen, and let dry completely.

Hanukkah Pops

Candles and color really make these shine. Add a decorative tag for a distinctive design.

YOU'LL NEED

48 uncoated Basic Cake Balls (page 11)

24 ounces white candy coating

2 deep, microwave-safe plastic bowls

48 six-inch white wax candles or paper lollipop sticks

White sugar crystals

2 large bowls

Wax paper

Baking sheet

24 ounces light blue candy coating

Blue sugar crystals

TO DECORATE

Have the cake balls chilled and in the refrigerator.

Melt the white candy coating in a microwave-safe plastic bowl, following the instructions on the package. The coating should be about 3 inches deep for easier dipping. (I usually work with about 16 ounces of coating at a time.)

When you are ready to dip, remove a few cake balls at a time from the refrigerator, keeping the rest chilled.

One at a time, dip about ½ inch of the bottom end of a candle in the melted white candy coating, and insert it straight into a cake ball, pushing it no more than halfway through. Dip half of the cake pops into the melted white coating, and tap off any excess coating, as described on page 36. Hold the wax candle close to the cake pop or it will bend when you tap it.

Immediately sprinkle white sugar crystals on each cake pop until it is covered completely. Sprinkle over a large bowl and you can catch and reuse any sprinkles that fall into it.

Place the cake pops, ball-side down, on a wax paper–covered baking sheet, and let dry completely.

Repeat with the remaining cake pops using the blue candy coating and blue sugar crystals.

Let dry completely.

note: Attach tags with tape for presentation, but make sure to remove them before you light the candles. You can download a PDF for these tags at www.bakerella.com/tags

Reindeer

Miniature pretzels make perfect reindeer antlers. Complete the look with red or dark brown candies for noses.

YOU'LL NEED

48 uncoated Basic Cake Balls (page 11)

48 ounces (3 pounds) chocolate candy coating

Deep, microwave-safe plastic bowl

48 paper lollipop sticks

96 miniature E-, F-, and Y-shaped alphabet pretzels

Styrofoam block

Toothpicks

48 brown M&M's, red Lemonheads, or red peanut M&M's

96 miniature white confetti sprinkles

Black edible-ink pen

TO DECORATE

Have the cake balls chilled and in the refrigerator.

Melt the chocolate candy coating in a microwave-safe plastic bowl, following the instructions on the package. The coating should be about 3 inches deep for easier dipping. (I usually work with about 16 ounces of coating at a time.)

When you are ready to dip, remove a few cake balls at a time from the refrigerator, keeping the rest chilled.

One at a time, dip about ½ inch of the tip of a lollipop stick into the melted candy coating, and insert the stick straight into a cake ball, pushing it no more than halfway through. Dip the cake pop into the melted coating, and tap off any excess coating, as described on page 36.

Immediately attach 2 pretzels on either side of each reindeer head for antlers. Hold them in place until the candy coating sets like glue, and let dry in the Styrofoam block.

Use a toothpick to dot a small amount of melted candy coating in position for the nose, and attach 1 brown or red candy. Hold in place until the coating sets.

Use a toothpick to dot a small amount of coating in position for the eyes, and attach 2 white miniature confetti sprinkles. Let dry completely in the Styrofoam block.

Draw mouths and dot the eyes with a black edible-ink pen. Let dry completely.

Tips

- If you can't find pretzels in alphabet shapes, just use mini or regular pretzel twists and break them in half for a pair of antlers.

- The antlers will be delicate. Be extra careful when transporting these.

Simple Santa Hats

These Santa hat cake pops make sweet stocking stuffers.

YOU'LL NEED

48 uncoated Basic Cake Balls (page 11), formed into cone shapes

16 ounces (1 pound) white candy coating

2 deep, microwave-safe plastic bowls

48 paper lollipop sticks

Styrofoam block

48 ounces (3 pounds) red candy coating

48 white chocolate–coated espresso beans

White sugar crystal sprinkles

Tip

- White gumballs and yogurt-covered peanuts will also work for the top of the hat.

TO DECORATE

Have the cake balls chilled and in the refrigerator.

Melt the white candy coating in a microwave-safe plastic bowl, following the instructions on the package.

When you are ready to dip, remove a few cake balls at a time from the refrigerator, keeping the rest chilled.

Hold the top part of the hat, and dip the bottom in the melted white coating, covering it about one-third of the way up. The top two-thirds of the hat will still be exposed. Insert a lollipop stick into the flat bottom of the hat. Place in the Styrofoam block to dry.

Melt the red candy coating in the second microwave-safe plastic bowl. The coating should be about 3 inches deep for easier dipping. (I usually work with about 16 ounces of coating at a time.) Dip the tops of the Santa hats in the red candy coating so that it meets the edge of the white coating.

Place an espresso bean on the top of the hat before the coating sets, and let dry completely in the Styrofoam block.

When the pops are dry, gently twist and remove the lollipop stick from the cake pop. Holding the pop by the top of the hat, redip the bottom in the melted white coating to make the coating thicker at the bottom. Then dip about ½ inch of the lollipop stick into the melted candy coating and insert it back into the bottom of the Santa hat. Sprinkle with white sugar crystals until the white candy coating is covered, and let dry completely in the Styrofoam block.

Cheery Christmas Trees

Use multicolored rainbow chip sprinkles to decorate Christmas tree cake pops. Top them off with jumbo star sprinkles.

YOU'LL NEED

48 uncoated Basic Cake Balls (page 11), formed into cone shapes

48 ounces (3 pounds) dark green candy coating

Deep, microwave-safe plastic bowl

48 paper lollipop sticks

Toothpicks

48 yellow jumbo star sprinkles

Styrofoam block

Multicolored rainbow chip sprinkles

TO DECORATE

Have the cake balls chilled and in the refrigerator.

Melt the green candy coating in a microwave-safe plastic bowl, following the instructions on the package. Make sure the bowl is filled deep enough with candy coating that you can submerge the entire cone-shaped cake pop in one dunk.

When you are ready to dip, remove a few cake balls at a time from the refrigerator, keeping the rest chilled.

One at a time, dip about ½ inch of the tip of a lollipop stick into the melted candy coating, and insert the stick straight into the flat bottom of a shaped cake ball, pushing it no more than halfway through. Dip the cake pop into the melted candy coating, and tap off any excess coating, as described on page 36.

Before the coating sets, use a toothpick to drag gently through the coating, creating branches. Just touch the toothpick on the wet coating and pull it away from the pop several times. You can also use the toothpick to apply more coating to the cake pop if necessary. Then place a jumbo star sprinkle on top of the tree.

Let dry completely in the Styrofoam block.

When the trees are dry, use a toothpick to apply dots of melted green candy coating to the tree in the places where you want ornaments, and attach multicolored rainbow chip sprinkles.

Let dry completely in the Styrofoam block.

Tip

- If you don't want branches, forget the toothpick and just go ahead and attach the rainbow chip sprinkles to the smooth surface of the tree-shaped cake pops.

Sweet Snowmen

Warm anyone's heart in the cold of winter with these cheerful treats.

YOU'LL NEED

48 uncoated Basic Cake Balls (page 11), formed into pear shapes

48 ounces (3 pounds) white candy coating

Deep, microwave-safe plastic bowl

48 paper lollipop sticks

48 orange candy-coated sunflower seeds

96 chocolate jimmies

Styrofoam block

Toothpicks

144 blue miniature confetti sprinkles

Black edible-ink pen

Small squeeze bottle

48 Murray Sugar-Free Chocolate Bites cookies

48 large dark chocolate chips, such as Ghirardelli

TO DECORATE

Have the pear-shaped cake balls chilled and in the refrigerator. Melt the white candy coating in a microwave-safe plastic bowl, following the instructions on the package. The coating should be about 3 inches deep for easier dipping. (I usually work with about 16 ounces of coating at a time.)

When you are ready to dip, remove a few cake balls at a time from the refrigerator, keeping the rest chilled.

One at a time, dip about ½ inch of the tip of a lollipop stick into the melted candy coating, and insert the stick straight into the bottom of a snowman body, pushing it no more than halfway through. Dip the cake pop into the melted coating, and tap off any excess coating, as described on page 36.

While the coating is still wet, attach a sunflower seed in position for the nose and 2 chocolate jimmies in position for the arms. Hold each in place for a few seconds until the candy coating sets like glue, then place in the Styrofoam block to dry. Repeat until all the snowmen have noses and arms.

When the pops are dry, use a toothpick to dot a small amount of melted candy coating in position for buttons and attach 3 blue confetti sprinkles to each snowman.

Draw on eyes and a dotted smile with an edible-ink pen and let dry completely in the Styrofoam block.

Pour the remaining melted coating into a small squeeze bottle. Squeeze a small amount onto the very top of a snowman's head. Attach 1 chocolate cookie. Squeeze another small amount of coating in the center opening of the cookie. Push 1 chocolate chip, pointed-side down, into the center. As you push, the melted candy coating will be forced up the side, giving you a white rim for the hat.

Place in the Styrofoam block to dry completely.

Cake & Frosting
recipes

It's a good idea to start out making cake pops using a box cake mix and ready-made frosting. The results are dependable, and there's no need to wonder if your homemade cake recipe makes the right amount of cake to accompany your homemade frosting recipe. The proportions are pretty perfect. Cake mixes are consistent that way, and that's why I like using them to make cake pops. But if you want to branch out beyond the box, here are a few basic recipes to get you started. These recipes yield about 60 cake balls or pops. Use them with one of the frosting recipes to maintain a good cake-to-frosting ratio when making cake balls. But feel free to experiment with your own cake and frosting recipes.

Cake Recipes

YELLOW CAKE

3 cups all-purpose flour (spooned and leveled)

2 teaspoons baking powder

½ teaspoon salt

1 cup butter, at room temperature

2 cups sugar

4 eggs, at room temperature

2 teaspoons vanilla extract

1 cup milk, at room temperature

Preheat the oven to 350 degrees F. Grease and flour a 9-by-13 inch cake pan.

In a large bowl, whisk together the flour, baking powder, and salt. Set aside.

Cream the butter and sugar with a mixer for 5 minutes, until light and fluffy.

Add the eggs, one at a time, to the creamed sugar and butter, mixing until just combined. Scrape down the sides of the bowl after each addition. Add the vanilla and mix until combined.

Add the flour mixture, a third at a time, alternating with the milk in two additions. (You'll begin and end with the flour mixture.)

Spread the batter (it will be thick) evenly into the prepared pan.

Bake for 35 to 40 minutes, or until a toothpick inserted in the center comes out clean.

Let the cake cool completely before crumbling for cake balls.

CHOCOLATE CAKE

2½ cups all-purpose flour (spooned and leveled)

1 cup unsweetened cocoa powder

1 teaspoon baking soda

2 teaspoons baking powder

½ teaspoon salt

1 cup butter, at room temperature

2 cups sugar

3 eggs, at room temperature

1 teaspoon vanilla extract

1½ cups milk, at room temperature

Preheat the oven to 350 degrees F. Grease and flour a 9-by-13 inch cake pan.

In a large bowl, whisk together the flour, cocoa powder, baking soda, baking powder, and salt. Set aside.

Cream the butter and sugar with a mixer for 5 minutes, until light and fluffy.

Add the eggs, one at a time, to the creamed sugar and butter, mixing until just combined. Scrape down the sides of the bowl after each addition. Add the vanilla and mix until combined.

Add the flour mixture, a third at a time, alternating with the milk in two additions. (You'll begin and end with the flour mixture.)

Spread the batter (it will be thick) evenly into the prepared pan.

Bake for 35 to 40 minutes, or until a toothpick inserted in the center comes out clean.

Let the cake cool completely before crumbling for cake balls.

Frosting Recipes

VANILLA FROSTING

$3/4$ cup butter, at room temperature

1 teaspoon vanilla extract

3 cups confectioners' sugar

1 to 2 teaspoons milk, if needed

Cream the butter and vanilla with a mixer until combined.

Add the sugar to the creamed mixture in two or three batches, scraping down the sides of the bowl after each addition.

If needed, add the milk to make the frosting creamier.

CREAM CHEESE FROSTING

6 tablespoons butter, at room temperature

6 ounces cream cheese, at room temperature

1 teaspoon vanilla extract

3 cups confectioners' sugar

Cream the butter and cream cheese with a mixer until combined.

Add the vanilla and mix until combined.

Add the sugar to the creamed mixture in two or three batches, scraping down the sides of the bowl after each addition.

CHOCOLATE FROSTING

$3/4$ cup butter, at room temperature

1 teaspoon vanilla extract

3 cups confectioners' sugar

$1/3$ cup unsweetened cocoa powder

1 to 2 teaspoons milk, if needed

Cream the butter and vanilla with a mixer until combined.

Add the sugar to the creamed mixture in two or three batches, scraping down the sides of the bowl after each addition.

Add the cocoa powder and mix until combined.

If needed, add the milk to make the frosting creamier.

CHOCOLATE CREAM CHEESE FROSTING

6 tablespoons butter, at room temperature

6 ounces cream cheese, at room temperature

1 teaspoon vanilla extract

3 cups confectioners' sugar

$1/3$ cup unsweetened cocoa powder

Cream the butter and cream cheese with a mixer until combined.

Add the vanilla and mix until combined.

Add the sugar to the creamed mixture in two or three batches, scraping down the sides of the bowl after each addition.

Add the cocoa powder and mix until combined.

Displaying, Storing Shipping & Supplies

So now you know how to make cake pops. But you may be wondering, "How am I going to present them?" Here are several approaches to try. From do-it-yourself displays to custom-built stands, there are many ways to help your cake pop creations shine like pop stars.

You can also use these tag designs to help your tiny treats make a big impression.

Visit www.bakerella.com/tags for downloadable designs.

DISPLAYING YOUR CAKE POPS

STYROFOAM BLOCKS: Used as a place to allow your cake pops to dry, they can also be covered in scrapbook paper for a pretty, easy, and inexpensive display. Measure your Styrofoam and cut a piece of paper to match the length and width of the block. Use plain paper for this, not decorative paper; it will serve as a template. Placing them 2 inches apart, make marks on the paper where the holes will be, using a pencil. Place the paper over the Styrofoam and poke through the paper at the marks with the tip of a pencil. Then mark each spot on the Styrofoam with a marker. Remove the paper and use a paper lollipop stick to poke holes into the Styrofoam. Try to insert the stick as straight into the Styrofoam as possible, without poking all the way through it. Wrap the Styrofoam block in decorative paper. Place the paper template on top of the wrapped Styrofoam and mark the hole locations with a pencil. This time, make a few tiny holes with the end of a needle, so you'll be able to insert the lollipop stick through without ripping the decorative paper. Be careful when removing cake pops from a Styrofoam block. If all the cake pops are removed from one side, the weight of the pops on the other side can cause the Styrofoam to tip over.

GLASSWARE: Glass dishes filled with sugar make an eye-pleasing display for cake pops. The sugar should be deep enough to keep the sticks standing upright. You can also fill deep glass dishes with gumballs, M&M's, or even marbles for a decorative approach. Glass candy dishes with lids are also a pretty way to display and store cake balls.

BOUQUETS: You can use a flowerpot or basket to display cake pops. Place a Styrofoam ball or block inside the basket so that it's secure. Then arrange the cake pops in the Styrofoam. You can disguise the Styrofoam ball by filling in around the sticks with paper confetti, ribbon, streamers, or some other fun decoration.

PAINTED WOOD DISPLAYS: You'll need a drill and a ruler for this one. Mark holes 2 inches apart on a piece of wood that is about 2 inches thick. Make a mark on the drill bit about 1¾ inches from the tip, so that you don't drill all the way through the wood. Drill a hole slightly larger than the diameter of the lollipop sticks you have chosen for a secure fit. Lighter wood with less grain will look the best. Use a drill bit slightly larger than the thickness of your lollipop stick.

LOLLIPOP STANDS: Super-cute premade displays are a great way to go if you're in a hurry. They're also called lollipop trees or sucker displays. Wilton.com carries a convenient lollipop and treat stand, and if you're feeling crafty you can make one (go to www.martha stewartweddings.com/article/lollipop-stand-how-to).

GIFT TAGS, TREAT BAGS, AND RIBBON: Individual cake pops make a great impression when given as gifts. Simply wrap each cake pop in a small plastic treat bag, and tie with decorative ribbon. You can make them even more special by including a sweet note. Use a 2- to 3-inch-wide paper punch, available in craft stores, and punch shapes out of heavyweight card stock. Then use a regular hole punch to make two holes on either side of the shape. Add a handwritten note, and slide the tag onto the lollipop stick. Or use a computer to typeset the message you want on card stock and use a large paper punch to punch around it. Or skip all of that and visit www.bakerella.com/tags for a few downloadable designs.

STORING AND SHIPPING CAKE POPS

Storage

Cake pops made with a cake mix and ready-made frosting can be stored in an airtight container on the counter. If you wrap them individually in treat bags tied with ribbon, they can stand in the Styrofoam block until ready to serve.

Cake pops made with homemade ingredients that are perishable, such as cream cheese frosting, should be stored in the refrigerator, either in an airtight container or wrapped in treat bags.

Cake pops will last for several days and can be made a few days before an event. The finished pops can also be stored in the freezer if you need to make them further in advance.

note: Manufacturers do not recommend storing candy coating in the refrigerator or freezer. But I have had success with storing the finished pops by wrapping in individual treat bags tied with a ribbon and placing them in an airtight container.

Shipping

Cake pops, bites, and balls are surprisingly easy to ship. Look for pastry boxes to place them in.

Cover cake pops with treat bags tied with ribbon, and then lay them in alternating directions in a small pastry or cake box. Use tissue paper to fill in any gaps and to keep the pops from sliding around in the box.

You can place cake balls and cupcake bites in paper or foil candy cups or use candy wrappers before mailing them in pastry boxes.

Tape the box shut and place it in a larger box surrounded by packing material. Ship them overnight to ensure freshness.

Supplies

Cake and Candy Making

Candy coatings, candy molds, lollipop sticks, treat bags, and more can be found at the following online sources.

- Cake Art: www.cakeart.com
- Candyland Crafts: www.candylandcrafts.com
- CK Products: www.ckproducts.com
- Confectionery House: www.confectioneryhouse.com
- Kitchenkrafts.com: www.kitchenkrafts.com

Candy

Grocery stores, drugstores, and even gas stations carry a wide assortment of candies to get your creative juices flowing. Here are a few online options as well.

- Candy Direct: www.candydirect.com
- Candy Warehouse: www.candywarehouse.com
- Dylan's Candy Bar: www.dylanscandybar.com
- M&M's: www.mms.com (purchase the color you want)

Candy Coatings

Chocolate, vanilla, and colored candy coatings are available from Merckens, Make 'n Mold, and Wilton. Chocolate and vanilla varieties are also available from the Kroger grocery store chain. Other brands available: Plymouth Pantry Almond Bark, Ambrosia Bark Coating, and Clasen Confectionery Coatings.

- Kroger: www.kroger.com
- Make 'n Mold: www.makenmold.com
- Merckens: available from cake and candy suppliers
- Wilton: www.wilton.com

Candy Coloring

- Chefmaster candy color: available from cake and candy suppliers
- Make 'n Mold: www.makenmold.com
- Wilton: www.wilton.com

Candy Molds

- CK Products: www.ckproducts.com (medium candy cup mold, product number: 90-5607; dome truffle mold, product number: 90-5651; disc mold, product number: 90-5022)
- Life of the Party: www.lifeofthepartymolds.com (medium candy cup mold, product number: AO032 ; Square mold, product number: AO107)

Candy Oil

- LorAnn Oils: www.lorannoils.com

Edible-Ink Pens

- Americolor: www.americolorcorp.com

Flower Cookie Cutters (for Cupcake Pops)

- Williams-Sonoma (available in a mini-cutter set in retail stores)
- Wilton (available in mini sets)
- Ateco (available in mini-cutter set number 4848)

Sprinkles (Shown on Cupcake Pops)

- Mr.Sprinkles: www.mr-sprinkles.com

Craft Stores

Retail craft stores also carry most of the basics you'll need for many of the projects.

- Jo-Ann Fabric and Craft Stores: www.joann.com
- Michaels: www.michaels.com
- Hobby Lobby: www.hobbylobby.com
- A.C. Moore: www.acmoore.com

Cake Pop Projects Photo Index

Page 49　Page 51　Page 53　Page 55　Page 57　Page 59　Page 61

Page 63　Page 67　Page 69　Page 73　Page 75　Page 77　Page 79

Page 81　Page 83　Page 85　Page 89　Page 91　Page 93　Page 95

Page 97　Page 99　Page 103　Page 105　Page 108　Page 111　Page 117

Page 119　Page 121　Page 123　Page 125　Page 127　Page 129　Page 131

Page 133　Page 135　Page 137　Page 139　Page 141　Page 143　Page 145

Index

A

Apple Pops, 75

B

Baby Faces, 81
Ball Cupcake Bites, Game, 97–98
Barnyard Friends, 105–7
Bears
 Brown Bears, 114
 Koala Bears, 117
 Panda Bears, 119
Bloom, 28
Bride and Groom Cake Pops, 79
Brown Bears, 114
Bunny Pops, Pastel, 55

C

Cake pops and cake balls. *See also individual projects*
 Basic Cake Balls, 11–12
 Basic Cake Pops, 15–16
 decorating, 42–45
 dipping, 36
 displaying, 152
 equipment for, 39, 40–41
 flavor combinations for, 30
 ingredients for, 40
 shaping, 32
 shipping, 154
 smaller numbers of, 31, 46
 storing, 154
 troubleshooting, 28

Cakes
 adapting homemade recipes for, 30
 Chocolate Cake, 148
 choosing, 40
 crumbling, 30
 Yellow Cake, 148
Candy coating
 buying, 40
 chocolate as substitute for, 28, 33
 colors of, 33, 34
 flavoring, 34
 melting, 33
 storing, 32
 thinning, 33
 troubleshooting, 28
 varieties of, 14, 32
Candy coloring, 40
Candy flavoring oils, 40
Candy molds, 41
Candy writers, 40
Cats, Black, 123
Chickens, 107
Chicks, Spring, 53
Chocolate
 as candy coating substitute, 28, 33
 Chocolate Cake, 148
 Chocolate Cream Cheese Frosting, 149
 Chocolate Cupcake Pops, 69–71
 Chocolate Frosting, 149
Christmas
 Cheery Christmas Trees, 143

Reindeer, 139
Simple Santa Hats, 141
Sweet Snowmen, 145
Clowning Around, 63–65
Cow Pops, 106
Cream cheese
Chocolate Cream Cheese Frosting, 149
Cream Cheese Frosting, 149
Cupcake pops and cupcake bites
Basic Cupcake Bites, 25–26
Basic Cupcake Pops, 19–22
Chocolate Cupcake Pops, 69–71
dipping, 36–37
Game Ball Cupcake Bites, 97–98
Pool Party Pops, 85–87

D
Dipping methods, 36–37
Display tips, 152

E
Easter
Confetti Easter Eggs, 59
Easter Baskets, 61–62
Pastel Bunny Pops, 55
Spring Chicks, 53
Equipment, 39, 40–41

F
Froggies, 103
Frostings
Chocolate Cream Cheese Frosting, 149

Chocolate Frosting, 149
choosing, 40
Cream Cheese Frosting, 149
Vanilla Frosting, 149

G
Game Ball Cupcake Bites, 97–98
Ghostly Goodies, 127
Graduation Caps, 83–84

H
Halloween
Black Cats, 123
Ghostly Goodies, 127
Jack-o'-Lanterns, 125
Owls, 133
Skulls, 127
Spooky Witches, 129
Yummy Mummies, 131
Hanukkah Pops, 137
Hearts, Sweet, 49

I
Ice Cream Cone Sundaes, 67–68

J
Jack-o'-Lanterns, 125

K
Koala Bears, 117

L

Ladybugs, Lovely Little, 99–101
Lions, Little, 111

M

Martians, 89
Monkey Business, 121
Monster Pops, 93
Mummies, Yummy, 131

O

Owls, 133

P

Panda Bears, 119
Paramount crystals, 40
Pens, edible-ink, 39, 40
Piggies, Pink, 105
Pirate Pops, 95
Pool Party Pops, 85–87
Popcorn Bags, 73
Puppy Pops, 108–10

R

Reindeer, 139
Robots, 91

S

Santa Hats, Simple, 141
Sheep, Sugar, 57
Shipping tips, 154

Skulls, 127
Snowmen, Sweet, 145
Spring Chicks, 53
Spring Fling, 51
Sprinkles, 42, 43
Storage tips, 154
Strawberry Patch Pops, 77
Supplies, 155
Sweet Hearts, 49

T

Thanksgiving
    Turkey Time, 135
Tigers, Tiny, 113
Toothpicks, 39, 41
Troubleshooting, 28
Turkey Time, 135

V

Valentine's Day
    Sweet Hearts, 49
Vanilla Frosting, 149

W

Weddings
    Bride and Groom Cake Pops, 79
Witches, Spooky, 129

Y

Yellow Cake, 148

Table of Equivalents

The exact equivalents in the following tables have been rounded for convenience.

LIQUID/DRY MEASUREMENTS

U.S.	Metric
¼ teaspoon	1.25 milliliters
½ teaspoon	2.5 milliliters
1 teaspoon	5 milliliters
1 tablespoon (3 teaspoons)	15 milliliters
1 fluid ounce (2 tablespoons)	30 milliliters
¼ cup	60 milliliters
⅓ cup	80 milliliters
½ cup	120 milliliters
1 cup	240 milliliters
1 pint (2 cups)	480 milliliters
1 quart (4 cups, 32 ounces)	960 milliliters
1 gallon (4 quarts)	3.84 liters
1 ounce (by weight)	28 grams
1 pound	448 grams
2.2 pounds	1 kilogram

LENGTHS

U.S.	Metric
⅛ inch	3 millimeters
¼ inch	6 millimeters
½ inch	12 millimeters
1 inch	2.5 centimeters

OVEN TEMPERATURE

Fahrenheit	Celsius	Gas
250	120	½
275	140	1
300	150	2
325	160	3
350	180	4
375	190	5
400	200	6
425	220	7
450	230	8
475	240	9
500	260	10